MONKEY
KUNG FU

MONKEY
KUNG FU

History & Tradition

by

6th Generation Grand Master
Michael Matsuda

DISCLAIMER

Please note that the publisher and author of this instructional book are NOT RESPONSIBLE in any manner whatsoever for any injury which may occur by reading and/or following the instructions herein.

It is essential that before following any of the activities, physical or otherwise, herein described, the reader or readers should first consult his or her physician for advice on whether or not the reader or readers should embark on the physical activity described herein. Since the physical activities described herein may be too sophisticated in nature, it is essential that a physician be consulted.

Dedication

To my wife Karen, my first and only sweetheart.
What an amazing inspiration you are and my
very best friend. And to my little Sparky who
brings such joy to my life.

To my parents who saw such great
potential in their son.
-- Michael Matsuda

Acknowledgements

To Sifu Lyle Fujioka, who took me under his
wing and became my first teacher.

To Grand Master Buck Sam Kong who opened
the doors of kung fu to so many and taught
me so much.

To the real "Monkey King,"
Monkey Grand Master Chan Sau Chung,
who keeps the art as pure as possible.

Preface

This is by far, the most accurate and detailed book on the history and traditions of the Northern Chinese art of Monkey kung fu. I have taken great care in documenting as much of the history as possible so that you, the reader, can learn all about this amazing art. I personally trained in this art for nearly 30 years and I am happy to share my experiences.

Through the lineage tracing back to Monkey kung fu founder, Grand Master Kou Sze, I have been charged with passing on all that I have learned so that others can keep this art alive.

Sadly, there are less than a handful of people who have completely mastered this rare art form. I am the only 6th Generation Monkey Grand Master and the only certified instructor in America who is actively teaching the art. Should anything adverse happen to me, the art would be completely lost to the American audience. Therefore, I have decided to document the entire Monkey system into detailed DVDs, books and a manual-type series.

Through this book, I will introduce you to the actual art as Grand Master Kou Sze designed it; as a fighting art, not a performance art.

You will learn a detailed history of the art as well as some additional information that you need to be aware of when learning this style. I have written this book with the intent of providing a thorough explanation of this art.

Lastly, though I am the author, I'm hesitant to write in the first person, so if you don't mind, the remainder of the book will be written in the third person.

Thank you and good reading.

6th Generation Grand Master Michael Matsuda

Table of Contents

Table of Contents

Chapter One

Introduction

Introduction

photo courtesy of Mario Prado

Monkey kung fu: It's without a doubt, the oddest form of fighting in the entire martial arts world. It's unorthodox, it's confusing, it's deceiving, it's comical, but more important, if learned correctly, it is brutally powerful.

The Monkey moves were originally designed to inflict great bodily pain within a quick burst of speed. Utilizing vital points, angled targets and deceptive attacks, the monkey finds an opportunity to strike with lethal force rendering its opponent helpless long enough for the monkey to get away.

However, to be blunt, Monkey kung fu is an extremely difficult Chinese art to learn, let alone, become a master of.

Most people usually only last a year in the art with the majority quitting after the first lesson. Only one out of several students in a class will continue in the art long enough to master it. Hence there was one student, Michael Matsuda, who continued long enough to completely master the entire system.

Monkey kung fu, also formerly called Tai Shing Pek Kwar kung fu, is a Northern Chinese art that was created around 1911.

It has been passed down from generation to generation. Only close friends or family members have been entrusted with the art. However, like in any artform, there are always exceptions.

This is not a technique book but a learning tool that will introduce you to the Monkey art of kung fu. It will dispel misconceptions, compare other monkey arts and provide some interesting facts that will assist those who wish to pursue the art and become a certified student or even a master.

Chapter Two

Meet Grand Master Matsuda

photo courtesy of Mario Prado

Meet 6th Generation Monkey Grand Master

Michael Matsuda

Grand Master Michael Matsuda is the only 6th Generation successor of the Northern Chinese art of Tai Shing (Monkey) kung fu and 8th Generation master of the art of Pek Kwar kung fu. He is only one of a handful of individuals in the world who have completely mastered the art and only the second non-Chinese to learn all five monkey forms. He is one of only two Americans who is fully certified by the United States Tai Shing Pek Kwar Association to teach the Monkey art. Sifu C.J. Martinez, Matsuda's student, has become the second.

Matsuda has authored over 50 articles on Monkey kung fu which has appeared in such magazines as *Inside Kung-Fu*, *Black Belt*, *Martial Art Magazine*,

photo courtesy of Hidy Ochiai

The Museum's Hall of Fame has become the most prestigious award in the martial arts industry. In 2004, the Martial Arts History Museum honored Master Michael Matsuda into their Hall of Fame for his contributions in opening the doors to Monkey Kung Fu to the West. Pictured are Hall of Fame inductees Bong Soo Han, John Corcoran, Byong Yu, Stephen Hayes and Michael Matsuda.

Inside Karate and more. He was the principal co-author of two Monkey kung fu books *(Monkey Kung Fu and History of Monkey Kung Fu)* and has graced the cover of six martial arts magazines. In 2004, he was inducted into the world's most prestigious Hall, the Martial Arts History Museum's Hall of Fame and is considered one of the primary pioneers opening the doors to Monkey kung fu in

America.

With over 40 years training in the martial arts, Matsuda has dedicated 30 years to learning and completely mastering the Monkey style. He is considered one of the leading authorities on the history of the Monkey art and continues to be the only master to be actively teaching the art in America.

In order to keep the traditions of the art as pure as possible, he has embraced the powerful striking aspects of the art as it was originally designed by the founder of the Monkey art, Grand Master Kou Sze.

It was during the 1980s, when the tournament circuit was at its height, a monkey competitor decided to add extreme flexibility and yoga moves to monkey "kata routines" in order to impress the judges. It worked, and he won a variety of tournaments. However, instead of removing the contortionist moves he added, he decided to teach them as authentic monkey postures.

Grand Master Matsuda has returned the art to its original core of Monkey fighting. To learn more about this unusual Monkey art, it's important that one learn a little about the master of the art.

The Beginning

From the beginning, Michael Gonzalez-Matsuda, a native of Southern California, was born in North Hollywood, a neighborhood located within the Los Angeles city limits.

The roots of his father's mother's side (Flores Family) can be accurately traced over 200 years. He is a direct descendent of California Governor Agustin

Zamorano and California Governor General Jose Maria Flores.

Zamorano was the first official printer in California and brought the first printing press to California. Today, a replica of this press can be found at the Printing Museum in California and a copy of one of his first printed books in California can be found at the California History Museum in Los Angeles, California.

Zamorano served his term of California Governor from 1831 through 1833. In addition to his political involvement, he was also an accomplished artist.

General Jose Maria Flores also served as Governor of Alta California from 1846 - 1847. A General in the Mexican army, Flores was best known for his successful battles against the American military. Originally from Mexico, he married into one of the founding families of California.

Self-portrait and signature of Agustin V. Zamorano

Agustin Zamorano was Governor of California from Dec. 1831-Jan. 1833. This is a self-portrait.

General Jose Maria Flores became a thorn in the American military's side as he continued to defy the Americans by winning a number of decisive battles against their stronghold. Flores was also appointed as Governor of Alta California from 1846-1847. The Flores Adobe in Pasadena, California is a historical monument and identifies the meeting place of Flores and his troops.

Martial Arts Roots

Michael's martial arts history began when he was around eight years old (this was in the late 1960s). As a skinny, scrawny young boy, he started getting picked on while in the fifth grade in elementary school. His father, Joe, took this as an opportunity to be proactive and began introducing Michael to some self-defense techniques, boxing drills and a few Japanese judo movements. Joe had learned a little judo from his friend when he was a young boy back in the 1920s. His friend's father happened to be a judo instructor.

Michael and his brother were forced by their father to take judo once a week at the Japanese Community Center (JACC) in Sun Valley, California. Though he hated every class, the techniques of the art came in handy when attacked by the school bully.

photo courtesy of Michael Matsuda

After a few months of training in their garage, Joe took Michael to the local Japanese Community Center (JACC) in Sun Valley, California and enrolled him in a judo class that they were offering. Joe had enrolled Michael's brother Richard in the same judo class one year earlier.

In the 1960s, judo was the most popular form of martial arts taught in America. Surfacing in the late 1800s and early 1900s, judo schools spanned its way across the nation and especially in California. Though Japanese karate was beginning to make its mark in the 1940s, it would be another 25 years until karate schools proliferated commercially. So, by default, judo schools dominated the arts in the United States.

The judo school at the community center, also called a dojo, was very, very traditional. The mats were made of straw; they felt like concrete when landed upon. All of the students were required to set up the dojo by laying out the mats in a traditional form before every class, and stacked them up after class.

There was only one color for the uniforms: eye-blinding white. All the instructions and phrases were in Japanese. Ninety-five percent of the students were pure Japanese, however, oddly enough, the chief instructor was a tall American with a white, butch-like haircut.

In total, there were about 40 students in the class which ranged in ages from 15 to 30 years. There were no small children in the class with the exception of Donald Isa and Michael who were both around eight years old.

Expecting a light introduction to the class, Michael's first day of judo was

This is the Japanese Community Center in Sun Valley, California. It is in this hall that Michael was first introduced to the Japanese art of judo. Ironically, it was the same hall some nine years later that Michael would first begin teaching Hung Gar kung fu.

photo courtesy of Michael Matsuda

a rude awakening. As soon as the opening bow was completed, the instructor grabbed him by the uniform and started performing every judo technique known to man on him. Tossed about like a rag doll, the instructor threw him all over the floor. From flips to throws, the instructor kept sweeping him every few seconds. Instead of waiting until Michael got up from the mat, he kept his hands on his uniform and picked him up only to throw him back down again in the next two seconds. The overbearing introduction to this traditional Japanese art lasted about 15 minutes but it seemed like an eternity to him.

Michael hated his first class and never wanted to return, but his father forced him to continue learning for a minimum of one year. So, every Tuesday night was dubbed "Nightmare Night" as he was nearly dragged to the judo class.

His only form of solace was working out with Donald Isa. Isa weighed about five pounds lighter than Michael and he turned out to be the only person he could actually flip with ease. And because they were the two youngest in the class, they were always paired together.

photo courtesy of Polytechnic High School

This is a high school picture of Donald Isa, but both he and Michael were about eight years old when they took Judo together at the JACC.

After a year-to-the-date arrived, Michael quit judo forever and ended his weekly nightmare. Even today, judo does not rank up there as a favorite martial art.

There was one instance, however, in which judo came to his aide. It was during the later half of the fifth grade at Arminta Street Elementary School in North Hollywood when Michael had an encounter with the school bully; we'll call him Michael Peterson (but that's not his real name). Peterson's method of intimidation was jumping on the backs of other school mates when they would lean slightly over to tie their shoe laces or to pick up something from the ground.

Peterson thought it was hilarious as he continued to bully the other classmates. One day, however, changed everything when Peterson decided to jump on Michael's back when he was in the middle of a game of dodgeball. Without an ounce of hesitation, Michael reached back, grabbed Peterson's right arm and executed a beautiful judo flip leaving Peterson on the ground with a stunned look on his face.

The whole class cheered and Peterson kept saying he fell on purpose but everyone knew better. That was the last day Peterson ever bothered Michael again. Though Michael still hated judo, it opened his eyes to the effectiveness of his martial arts training.

photo courtesy of Arminta School

It was here at the North Hollywood Arminta Street Elementary School that Michael first used his martial arts skill to defeat the bully of the school by using a judo flipping technique.

Moving On

Hoping to receive a more positive experience in the martial arts, Michael's mother enrolled him, his brother and their friend David Husson in a local karate school in Sherman Oaks, California headed by instructor Bob Ozman. Since Michael was still relatively young, there was a picture on the wall of Ozman fighting a tiger that impressed him the most.

photo courtesy of CDC Comics

Michael was a huge comic book fan in the 60s and his favorite comic was ironically a judo stylist called "Judo Master".

Sadly, the day before their first lesson, his friend David, broke his collar bone and was unable to start training but Michael and his brother continued learning the art.

For Michael, it was a welcome change from being thrown around every Tuesday night and it began to reveal to him that there were other arts which he could explore.

Sensei Bob Ozman was the chief instructor of the karate studio in Sherman Oaks in which Richard and Michael studied at..

After a time, his brother, Richard, decided to explore another type of Japanese martial art called jiu jitsu. He enrolled in a class given at the San Fernando Recreation Center in Fernangeles park. Michael decided to dabble in a few classes in the art as well.

Sadly, jiu jitsu seemed to be closer to the movements of the judo art, so Michael knew training in this course was going to end very quickly.

However, it was during one of the classes that Michael's destiny was unveiled when a young man named Al Dacascos came to visit his friend at the recreation center.

Dressed all in black with a high-colored uniform, Al and his friend began showing a few sparring techniques to the class.

Al's movements were circular and agile, his stances were low and his movements were flowing and very different from anything Michael had ever seen before.

The Japanese art of judo was actually developed from aspects of jiu jitsu by 2002 Museum Hall of Famer and pioneer Jigoro Kano.

Michael was so impressed by Al's movements that it was that moment in time that changed his life forever and he knew instantly, this was the type of martial art he was going to study for the rest of his life.

Dacascos was introduced to the class as an instructor in a Chinese art called kung fu. Kung fu was not openly available to non-Chinese until the early 1960s.

Unfortunately, finding a commercial kung fu school was nearly impossible even in the 1970s. But, Michael had a cousin named Emily who lived in downtown North Hollywood near Lankershim and Magnolia. Emily's home had a lot of bedrooms and to generate some additional income, she would rent out the rooms to college students. Her son, Manuel was going to college so he was able to bring in fellow students to fill up the rooms.

One of the tenants, named Juan, happened to know some kung fu. He was one of the few, lucky people who was able to train under a Chinese kung fu instructor and because he and Michael became friends, he would teach him some of the new techniques he learned every time Michael came to visit.

Formal Training

It was on the eve of attending Polytechnic High School in Sun Valley, California that Michael's mother Julia, found an article in the Valley News about a new kung fu class that was opening at the Mid-

photo courtesy of Sifu Al Dacascos

Sifu Al Dacascos, pictured here in 1972, visited his friend at a park community center and Michael became fascinated by his movements. It was then Michael decided to make kung fu his ambition.

Valley YMCA.

Michael's first formal class was held on September 15, 1973 at 10 am. This would be a date that would be precious to Michael for the rest of his life. The instructor's name was Sifu Warren, a Chinese practitioner who studied Hung Gar kung fu.

As he expected, the first class was more than amazing and it was exactly the art form he had spent his young life looking for. The fluid movements, the offensive and defensive techniques fit his body type perfectly and he knew at that moment that he had come home.

Altogether, there were about 20 people who showed up for the first day and three of them became Michael's

The Mid Valley YMCA was introducing a new program, the Chinese art of kung fu. Michael joined on the first day in 1973. On the left is a photograph of Mike Oda and a few of the fellow students ready to begin their first day of training.

photo courtesy of Mid Valley YMCA

closest friends: Sol Avery, Mike Oda and Robbie.

Michael's mother was a seamstress so she made him a black cotton uniform with white trim. He felt great pride wearing an actual kung fu uniform to class.

After several months of training, one Saturday morning Sifu Warren did not show up for class and another Chinese instructor stood in his place. His name was Sifu Brian.

Sifu Brian also studied Hung Gar kung fu and was

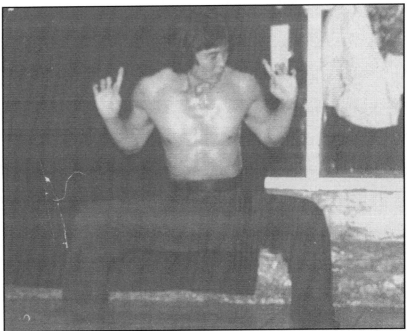

photo courtesy of Michael Matsuda

Sifu Lyle Fujioka became Michael's biggest influence in the martial arts world. This is a picture of Lyle Fujioka taken by Michael during a demonstration at the Hollywood school.

the cousin of one of Michael's high school friend, Jamie Inouye. Sifu Brian was a very good instructor but sadly he only taught for about two months.

His third instructor became the most influential martial arts individual in Michael's life. His name was Sifu Lyle Fujioka and he was a senior student at Sifu Buck Sam Kong's Siu Lum P'ai school in Hollywood. Sifu Lyle had a strong build and his kung fu was quite powerful. The style he taught was a combination of

Solomon Avery, pictured here, was considered the most senior student of the group because of his great skill in kung fu.

Choy Li Fut and Hung Gar kung fu (also called gung fu). Sifu Kong had a string of schools in Hawaii and the Hollywood school was run by his pupil, Sifu Vernon Rieta.

Sifu Lyle took the art very seriously and didn't let anyone proceed to the next movement until it could be performed perfectly. Whenever Sifu Lyle needed to demonstrate a technique for the class, he would always call Michael up front to be the dummy. Michael felt that it was an honor to be selected.

Pictured here was the original Buck Sam Kong Hollywood school on the corner of Kenmore and Hollywood Blvd. Ara's pastry shop stands there today.

After a time, Sol, Mike, Robbie and Michael became Sifu Lyle's primary students. Even though new people came and went, it was these four students that continued in the art.

After about a year of training at the YMCA, Sifu Lyle felt that his students were now skilled enough to begin attending the main kung fu school in Holly-wood. All jumped at the chance and agreed to show up at the main school the following Monday. Unfortu-nately, Robbie didn't make it to the class.

On the following Saturday YMCA class, Robbie didn't show up either. To their dismay, Robbie was never seen again.

About a month later, Sol brought a friend to the class named Chuck

photo courtesy of Grand Master Buck Sam Kong

Grand Master Buck Sam Kong took charge over his Hollywood school when he decided to move his family to the mainland. This is Master Buck Sam Kong in 1973.

Childers. Chuck became a faithful student and joined the rest at the Hollywood school as well.

For the next year, the four students continued to train at both the YMCA and the Hollywood school. Enrollment, however, at the YMCA declined and Sifu Lyle was forced to close the Saturday class.

Soon thereafter, Chuck stopped training altogether and Sol, who was

Master Michael Matsuda (upper right) and is shown here practicing at the Hung Gar (Siu Lum Pai) kung fu studio in 1979 in Hollywood, California on the corner of Kenmore and Hollywood Boulevard. The floor of the school was made of smooth, hard concrete and their pools of sweat caused them to fall many times. Sifu Vernon Rieta (above center) ran the school until Sifu Buck Sam Kong came to the mainland to take over.

photo courtesy of Polytechnic High School

Along with many friends, Michael played a role in developing the Asian American Student Association sponsored by teacher Gail Nitta. Gail would later train with Michael at the Hollywood school. Circled left to right are kung fu students Karen Matsuda Gonzalez, Laurie Baggao, Master Michael Matsuda and one of Michael's first two students, Bob Niitsuma.

considered the most senior of the four, got into a devastating car accident and was paralyzed. Oda and Michael pushed on, continued at the school and particularly excelled at the two-man hand forms.

In their third year of training, Mike Oda decided to leave the school and Michael alone remained as the last student left of the original four-man team.

Though his training was now focused at the main school, Sifu Lyle would continually pull Michael aside to teach him additional movements and correct his techniques.

Gail Nitta

Sifu Lyle became instrumental in developing Michael as a successful martial artist.

Throughout his entire time at high school, Michael was living and breathing kung fu. As soon as he woke up, he practiced, at school he practiced, when

he got home, he practiced and when he went to the Hollywood school he practiced with the beginners before his regular class.

Michael was lucky enough to befriend a high school teacher named Gail Nitta. Gail helped him

photo courtesy of Polytechnic High School

John H. Frances Polytechnic High School in Sun Valley, California where Michael attended.

and a host of other school mates (namely Liza Javier, Doris Isa, Karen Murakami

Bob Niitsuma became one of Michael's first two students.

and more) to create the Asian American Student Association (AASA) of Poly High School. Gail also loved the martial arts and she allowed to him to work out in her classroom during lunch.

In his senior year Michael helped form a martial arts club called the "Hop Sing Tong." The name had no meaning but it sounded cool; never realizing there was a real Hong Sing Tong society in the Los Angeles Chinatown.

Sonny Iwami

There were about 40 to 50 martial artists in the club. It wasn't an official club and they didn't really have any type of agenda, they just practiced a little bit and discussed martial arts. They met at lunch and the school would beef up their security as they watched them work out together.

During this time, Michael had developed a following and was already teaching some of his classmates Chinese kung fu. Sonny Iwami and Bob Niitsuma became his closest friends and his first two students.

Sonny was very popular so he got into all the Japanese events and Bob was very smart and he knew the answers to everything. Both were great guys that became instrumental in Michael's life.

In just a very short time, Michael had already gained over 30 students and was teaching them on a regular basis. Even Gail Nitta became one of his regular students.

This is a photograph of just some of Michael's students back in the late 1970s.

Gail also wanted to attend the Hollywood school so she would pick Michael up at his house and they would drive to the studio together (Michael didn't have his driver's license yet). Gail continued to study for about a year.

To expand his teaching potential, Michael made an arrangement with the Sun Valley Japanese Community Center to utilize their hall to teach his 30 students (the same dojo that he first began his study of judo).

It was also during this time that Michael also began learning a different and unusual type of

photo personally given to Michael

Grand Master Chan Sau Chung is the 3rd generation successor and the only living Grand Master of Monkey kung fu. This photograph was taken in front of his Hong Kong School and was autographed and given to Michael in 1976 after one of his demonstrations.

Chinese kung fu called Tai Shing Pek Kwar, or better known as Monkey style kung fu.

Michael had befriended a new student at the Hung Gar school and because they got along so well, Michael took him under his wing and started teaching him on the side in order for him to reach his level a little quicker so they could work out together.

He trained with him before and after every class trying to bring him up to speed. It was during this time that his friend decided to share a unique form of kung fu that he was learning called Monkey kung fu.

Michael was already familiar with Monkey kung fu because Sifu Buck Sam Kong assigned Michael as one of the escorts to the Monkey King, Chan Sau Chung at an East West performance.

Grand Master Chan was an extremely gifted master, who came to America in the 1970s to demonstrate Monkey and bring his stable of kickboxers.

Though Michael was still relatively young, he joined a number other escorts as they went with Grand Master Chan to his many demonstrations. Grand Master Chan was very strong and powerful and so were his students.

Grand Master Chan Sau Chung is the only living third gener-

flyer courtesy of Master Buck Sam Kong

BUCK SAM KONG'S EAST-WEST KUNG FU EXHIBITION

SEE KUNG FU at its BEST

DIRECT FROM HONG KONG

★ Featuring the one and only "Monkey King" CHAN SOU CHUNG and his team of tournament champions. Chan Sou Chung - Movie Star - Kung Fu Master of the Monkey Axe Style (Tai Sing Pek Kwar) - Trainer of Champions.

★ MASTER YEW CHING WONG from San Francisco with his deadly double chain whip.

★ By special request Master of Tiger Crane Style (Hung Gar System) MASTER LAM CHUN FAI from Hong Kong, son of GRAND MASTER LAM JO demonstrating the Double Sword set.

★ Exhibition sponsored by MASTER BUCK SAM KONG of Hawaii and his unbeatable 3-section staff.

SPONSORED BY EAST-WEST PROMOTIONS

This is the actual flyer in 1974 in which Grand Master Chan Sou Chung, the real "Monkey King" came to America with his stable of full-contact champions. Grand Master Chan Sau Chung kept the traditions of the art as a fighting system and proved it in the ring with a number of championships.

photo courtesy of Michael Matsuda

This is the actual uniform that Michael wore when he first began to learn Monkey kung fu. The boots were from Hong Kong in which he paid $80 for back in the 80s. The uniform evolved into an all back crepe satin uniform. However, on occasion he would wear a satin outfit with gold trim.

ation master of the art of Tai Shing. He is the only individual to rightfully carry the title "Monkey King."

The Chinese instructor, which taught Michael's classmate, was teaching the traditional way; Pek Kwar kung fu first, then Tai Shing kung fu. Therefore, neither Michael nor his classmate knew they were studying Monkey until much later. As the friend learned, Michael learned and became his first and eldest Monkey kung fu student.

After a few more years, Michael left the

Hung Gar school but continued studying the Monkey kung fu art. He also dabbled in a few interesting styles including Bruce Lee's art of Jeet Kune Do.

Michael had enrolled in a class to learn Mandarin Chinese with a Chinese community group in Northridge. The class was two hours but had a one hour break or alternative class in between. One of Dan Inosanto's student was teaching Jeet Kune Do. So for two years, Michael learned Chinese and kung fu.

Another area of training that helped mold

6TH GENERATION MASTER
MICHAEL MATSUDA

Monkey
KUNG FU

VOLUME 3: THE FORTY KICKS

photo courtesy of Mario Prado

The DVDs produced by Master Matsuda hold true to Monkey kung fu as a fighting art, the way it was meant to be taught. To keep this art from being lost or distorted, he is putting the complete Tai Shing system on DVD and in book form so that anyone all over the world can learn and possibly master the art..

Michael considerably was working out with former full-contact karate champion and 2003 Museum Hall of Famer Cecil Peoples.

Over the next several years, Peoples opened Michael's eyes to kickboxing training and sparring. The routine was grueling but it helped lay a foundation for strong and powerful workouts.

Peoples was one of the top rated full-contact fighters of his generation. His lightning fast speed, his powerful punches and his no-nonsense sweeps made him a feared champion.

When Michael began hosting tournaments, Peoples, along with close

Another inspiring individual in Michael's life was Sensei Cecil Peoples. Though kung fu is an excellent fighting art, it was Cecil who introduced Michael to unique training routines to work on his endurance.

Cecil would become one of Michael's most closest friends and would help him coordinate all his tournaments. Cecil was inducted into the Museum's Hall of Fame in 2003 for his accomplishments in helping to pioneer full-contact karate in America..

friend Fariborz Azhakh, would assist Michael in coordinating and running the events.

After 30 years of intense training, Michael succeeded his friend and became the 6th Generation Master of the art of Monkey kung fu.

Mastering all five forms of the Monkey, Michael became only the second non-Chinese to completely master the complete and entire artform.

Through the years, Michael became a pioneer for the art by introducing the Monkey style to the American public through a host of seminars, demonstrations, shows, numerous articles,  books, videos and DVDs.

Kung fu Master Dave Burgett of Valencia Martial Arts opened the doors to teaching Monkey kung fu commercially.

In 2005, Michael was honored by the Martial Arts History Museum by being inducted into its Hall of Fame for his pioneering accomplishments in spreading the art to the West. His uniform and staff are proudly displayed at the museum.

In 2006, kung fu school owner and instructor Master Dave Burgett invited Michael to begin teaching the Monkey kung fu style to the public. Michael agreed. He discontinued his private classes

Extreme flexibility has never been a part of actual Tai Shing. However, Master Matsuda takes a moment to perform a splits stretch at a garage school back in the 1980s.

This photo was taken by a timer by Master Matsuda.

and began teaching the art commercially for Master Burgett at Valencia Kung Fu in the city of Santa Clarita, California.

Because the art of Pek Kwar kung fu has nothing to do with Tai Shing kung fu (which you will learn about in the following chapters), Michael has been introducing his students to the Monkey art only. By the time this book is printed, one of his students (C.J. Martinez), will be only the third American to master three of the five monkey forms and promoted to the rank of Sifu.

In addition to formal instruction, Master Matsuda began producing a complete series of DVDs, workbooks, historical books and more on learning the complete Monkey kung fu art.

For Michael, it's so vital, especially now,

Mr. Fariborz Azhakh helped Michael considerably through the years. They became extremely close friends and have owned a number of businesses together.

that this art be shared with the rest of the world. There are only a handful of people in the world that have mastered this art and if it isn't passed on in some form, it will be easily lost.

In addition, Grand Master Matsuda stresses the importance to learn the art correctly rather than learning a performance or watered down art. This is a very traditional art that is only a century old, but without proper instruction, it can be and in some cases, has been easily distorted.

photo courtesy of Marc Lawrence

Master Matsuda demonstrating a monkey front kick while at the Museum.

It is Grand Master Michael Matsuda's goal to open this secretive art form to the entire world. The five monkey forms, which are known to only four individuals, will now be available for all to learn and master.

One individual that Michael holds in very high regard is Fariborz Azhakh. Azhakh is the chief instructor of Team Karate Centers in Woodland Hills, CA. Because of his assistance over several decades, he has opened doors for Michael to produce a number of Monkey seminars, training sessions, workshops and more. Azhakh met Michael when he became heavily involved in tournament competition. Azhakh was listed as one of the top ten forms competitors in the region.

Summary

Now you know how it all started. Hung Gar kung fu is my first love in the arts and always will be. Although I spent nearly 35 years devoted to mastering Monkey kung fu, the best years of my life and the most enjoyable were training under Sifu Lyle Fujioka and Sifu Buck Sam Kong. They were more than great instructors, they were my mentors.

Chapter Three

Defining the Arts

Defining the arts of
Monkey Style Kung Fu

Monkey style kung fu. It is rarest and most secretive style of fu. Though many may be familiar form, they tend to share a common believing that there is only one Monstyle when in fact, there are three. One thousands of years old and another is 100 years old.

perhaps, the Chinese kung with this art misconception; key kung fu of them is only a mere

They include:

Shaolin Monkey

Wu Shu Monkey

Tai Shing Pek Kwar Monkey

Shaolin Monkey

The Shaolin Temple is generally considered by many as the birth place of the martial arts. It has been said that the temple monks devised the art of kung fu from the unique characteristics of the animals surrounding the temple.

As a result, the monks were able to create a number of interesting and effective styles including the Tiger, Crane, Leopard, Snake and Dragon which make up today's five animal system.

In addition to these five, a variety of other animals styles were created including the playful, yet powerful style of the Shaolin Monkey.

Designed to be confusing and unorthodox, the Shaolin Monkey was a different type of art that required a unique

Shaolin Monkey is the oldest of all three monkey styles. The Shaolin Temple, pictured here, is considered the focal point of the martial arts.

photo courtesy of Master Seming Ma

personality.

Though it is safe to assume that the Shaolin Monkey was probably developed in the same era as the five animal styles, the Shaolin Monkey was overshadowed by the more prominent art forms. As a result, the new-found monkey art quickly was in jeopardy in finding itself extinct.

Thankfully, the art continued and was passed down from generation to generation to anyone who would seek an interest in learning.

The late Grand Master Ark Y. Wong was considered the leading authority for Shaolin Monkey in America. Also a master of the Five Animal System, Grand Master Wong helped continue the family line of this unusual art.

Unfortunately, there was such little interest in learning the Shaolin Monkey that Grand Master Wong rarely taught the monkey style, but, thanks to the innovation of film, he kept the art alive by recording it on 8mm film so that others can learn and master the Monkey art. A special thanks goes to Grand Master Douglas Lim Wong for also recording Grand Master Ark Y. Wong's performances.

Masters Douglas Lim Wong and Carrie Ogawa-Wong, both museum hall inductees, keep the tradition of the five animal system alive through their White Lotus kung fu school.

Shaolin Monkey kung fu was designed as a combative style of art, it was never intended to be flashy or showy. To fight against other warriors, it had to be

(Left) Grand Master Ark Y. Wong is credited as the "father of kung fu in America." He is one of the few individuals who actually learned the Shaolin Monkey art. Today, many of his students carry on the art including Douglas Lim Wong, his grandson Seming Ma, A. A. Velazquez and many more.

strong and highly effective. The movements are not as low to the ground as other monkey styles, but it shares techniques of deception and unorthodox striking and punching.

Though the rolling, jumping and leaping movements mimic the carefree monkey, the Shaolin Monkey was designed to resemble a more human-like form.

Grand Master Doug Wong

photo courtesy of White Lotus Kung Fu

About Grand Master Ark Y. Wong

Grand Master Wong was considered by many as the "father of kung fu in America." He was the first acknowledged individual to begin publicly teaching kung fu to the non-Chinese community. He became a pioneer for his efforts and as a result, influenced the entire world. In 2006, the late Grand Master Wong was honored by being inducted into the Museum's Hall of Fame.

Wu Shu Monkey

Clearly the most unique and dynamic of the three monkey styles is the Wu Shu Monkey. It is filled with artistic movements, acrobatic techniques, free flowing motions and awesome flexibility. It is without a doubt, the most popular of the three.

Though the Shaolin and Tai Shing monkey's primary focus is fighting, the goal of the Wu Shu Monkey is performance and demonstration. Though many of

The Chinese monks provide beautiful performances across America using Wu Shu kung fu. Wu Shu monkey hand forms and staff forms are always a treat.

its movements can be effective if applied appropriately; that is not the goal of the Wu Shu form.

One of the more interesting aspects of Wu Shu Monkey is its duo-role of performing in the Chinese opera.

Equipped with additional flashy acrobatics, impressive lighting fast speed and unusual postures, the Opera monkey is an amazing performance to enjoy.

The Opera Monkey, when used in the Chinese opera, convincingly portrays the role of the "Monkey King", Sun Wu Kong in the traditional and revered folklore, "Journey to the West."

Wu Shu Monkey is so popular it is demonstrated regularly by the Shaolin Monks performing groups. The movements are both high and low postures and mimic the facial expressions and monkey mentality. In addition to its hand form, the Wu Shu Monkey incorporates a silver staff form that will dazzle any competitor with its speed and accuracy.

The staff form is used in both Wu Shu and Opera monkey performances.

Wu Shu and Opera monkey wear a similar type of uniform, however, Opera is a little more elaborate and the face is painted to resemble an actual monkey.

The Wu Shu Monkey is widely available for study throughout the world.

One of the trademarks shared by both the Wu Shu and Chinese opera Monkey is that its practitioner uses the staff as a ladder and climbs to the top to look over the horizon.

Tai Shing Pek Kwar Monkey

The third and final style of Monkey kung fu is called Tai Shing Pek Kwar. It is the youngest of the three which was developed just over 100 years ago.

The style was created by one individual, Kou Sze, who adapted the characteristics of monkeys into another Chinese art called; Tei Tong or Great Earth style.

In a nutshell, it is a pure and powerful fighting art. The movements are strong and hard and its techniques are quick and deadly. Though many of its movements are comical, with a lot of rolling and low maneuvering, it was never designed as a showmanship artform.

Tai Shing Pek Kwar is all about defeating the opponent with force, strength and cunningness. It does not contain any extreme flexibility or yoga postures.

The Tai Shing Pek Kwar art is divided into five different monkey forms; 1) Lost, 2) Tall, 3) Stone, 4) Drunken and; 5) Wooden.

photo courtesy of Mario Prado

The first generation of Tai Shing Pek Kwar began with Grand Master Kou Sze in the early 1900s. Since then, it has progressed to America with Grand Master Michael Matsuda succeeding as the sixth generation Grand Master.

The art has been passed down from generation to generation; from family to family and friends to friends. Because there are only a handful of individuals who have mastered the art, it is extremely difficult to find a certified instructor.

Summary

As you can see, three different arts were created called Monkey style kung fu. Though Shaolin Monkey was created within the walls of Shaolin, it took much longer to understand and a result, more time to be effective. Therefore, other Shaolin styles such as Tiger and Crane became more popular. That is why the monkey art nearly faded away.

Wu Shu Monkey was developed from the Opera monkey from the theatrical play of "Journey to the West." When Wu Shu was created and adapted by the Shaolin Temple, the Wu Shu Monkey was born. Unfortunately, we don't have an exact timeframe when the transition occurred.

Tai Shing Monkey was developed from the Great Earth style by Kou Sze. Made completely out of boredom, the style consisted of powerful fighting moves and techniques. He named the art after the Monkey King, Sun Wu Kong who also goes by the name of Great Sage when he became an immortal.

Explaining Tai Shing Pek Kwar Kung Fu

Another common misconception that most people never seem to realize is that there is actually no such thing as Tai Shing Pek Kwar kung fu. The book does utilize the term Tai Shing Pek Kwar, but in reality, Tai Shing is one kung fu style all in itself, and Pek Kwar is a separate kung fu style as well.

Explanation:

The words "Tai Shing" in Chinese means "Great Sage."

This refers to the Monkey King, Sun Wu Kong from the Chinese folklore "Journey to the West." He was also referred to as the "Great Sage" when he reached immortality. Tai Shing are the only words in this group that actually represent the term, Monkey kung fu.

The words "Pek Kwar" in Chinese means "Axe Fist"

This refers to another completely different style of kung fu called Axe Fist style. Very similar to Choy Li Fut kung fu, the style uses arm-swinging motions which are positioned as if holding an axe in each hand.

Pek Kwar has nothing to do whatsoever with Tai Shing kung fu. It has no foundation for the art, it doesn't share any of the techniques, nor does it help prepare someone to study the Monkey art.

In reality, it is the art of Tei Tong, or Great Earth style, that has more in common with Monkey kung fu than Pek Kwar.

The Combination of Terms

As noted previously, the actual style of Monkey kung fu or Tai Shing was created by a Great Earth kung fu stylist named Grand Master Kou Sze. By combining the movements of the monkey along with the foundation of the Great Earth style, he invented the art of Monkey kung fu which he called, Tai Shing.

Grand Master Kou Sze had one and only student that we know of, Grand Master Ken Tak Hoi. Grand Master Ken Tak Hoi was already an extremely accomplished master of a Chinese art called Pek Kwar or Axe Fist.

However, when Grand Master Ken Tak Hoi began instructing others, he didn't want to teach Tai Shing to just anyone so he jealously hid the Monkey art and openly taught Pek Kwar. But, to those he felt were worthy enough, he introduced them to the art of Monkey kung fu.

Grand Master Ken Tak Hoi was the 4th Generation master of Pek Kwar and 2nd Generation master of Tai Shing.

It was at this time he decided to combine the two names into one and called his school Tai Shing Pek Kwar kung fu; two different arts that are taught at the same location.

Over the years, however, people kept referring Tai Shing Pek Kwar as just a single art form rather than two distinct and effective arts.

Summary

For clarification, Tai Shing is the actual Monkey kung fu art form. Grand Master Kou Sze only taught the Monkey art. He never knew Pek Kwar kung fu.

Pek Kwar kung fu is an arm-swinging kung fu artform very similar to Choy Li Fut kung fu. It has nothing whatsoever in common with Tai Shing. It doesn't share a single kick, movement nor technique.

Grand Master Matsuda has chosen to only teach the Tai Shing art and discontinue teaching Pek Kwar. However, because this is a book on history, the next two chapters will provide a brief background on Pek Kwar. The remainder of the book will focus on Tai Shing (Monkey) kung fu only.

Chapter Four

The History of Pek Kwar

The History of

Pek Kwar
Kung Fu

Pek Kwar kung fu is a Northern
Chinese artform that was developed over 200
years ago by a kung fu practitioner named Grand Master Ma
Chi Ho. Though most kung fu styles are based on animal
movements and characteristics, Pek Kwar is just the opposite. Its
foundation is focused more on human capabilities.

The history of Pek Kwar, or "Axe Fist" style, begins with the story
about a young, good-hearted man who lived in a village near Shantung Province,
China. To gather firewood, young Ma Chi Ho would travel just outside the
village to a forest which was filled with trees.

There was a temple located just down the road from the forest and out of
the kindness of his heart, he would cut down some extra firewood and bring it to
the monks at the temple.

Ma Chi Ho was a thick, strong man so he chose to use a short axe to cut down the branches. In time, he became so skilled at cutting with the small axe, that he was able to knock down a branch with just one swing. To double his efforts, he would occasionally use an axe in each hand and with a one-two striking motion, chopping down two branches simultaneously. This double-striking motion would later become the foundation for developing the Pek Kwar style.

As time went on, Ma became acquainted and quite friendly with some of the monks at the temple. Noticing Ma's two handed swinging motion, one of the monks approached him and picked up

one of the axes. He examined the axe carefully and said to Ma, "Metal may conquer wood." Ma replied, "Yes, it does."

To demonstrate, Ma picked up the axe, swung it at a branch, knocked it down and brought it to the monk and said, "Yes, you are correct, metal conquers wood."

The monk then put his finger on Ma's chest and said, "But the spirit is stronger." Ma replied, "I don't understand." Without any further explanation, the monk just turned and walked back to the temple.

Ma Chi Ho contemplated the monk's unusual phrase but he didn't fully understand its meaning.

A few weeks had passed and the same monk came up to Ma and said, "Metal may conquer wood," and immediately Ma picked up the axe and was ready to strike off another branch. The monk took the axe from his hand and set it down and again pointed at Ma's heart and finished his saying, " but the spirit is stronger." The monk closed Ma's fist and brought it down to the branch

As Grand Master Matsuda began learning more advanced Pek Kwar forms, it became very evident that Pek Kwar had nothing whatsoever to do with the Monkey art. It was then Matsuda decided to discontinue practicing Pek Kwar and spend more time focusing on Tai Shing forms and routines. Here, Master Matsuda is pictured with student Luke Walden. This is the last time Matsuda used Pek Kwar.

and again said to him, "the spirit is stronger."

Ma replied, "you want me to knock the branch down with just my arm?" and the monk replied, "Allow your inner spirit, your chi to knock down the branch."

After a period of time, the monk taught Ma how to breathe properly and cultivate his energy. When young Ma felt he was prepared enough, he approached the tree, lifted his arm and allowed the energy to flow through his arm and in one swift motion, knocked down the branch.

He turned to the monk and said, "but the spirit is stronger." The monk smiled and walked away.

As months passed,

Grand Master Ken Tak Hoi was the 4th Generation master of Pek Kwar and 2nd Generation master of Tai Shing.

Ma became just as proficient in chopping branches with his arms as with his axes. In time, Ma would incorporate a variety of stances and different approaches to swinging and slicing.

Through a series of motions and movements, Ma created a new form of kung fu he called Pek Kwar, or Axe-Fist style, because it represented a person holding an axe in each hand. Though the art wasn't as circular as most Chinese styles, it was still very effective and powerful.

Later, Ma Chi Ho began to teach his new-found art openly. One of his students was Ken Ming Kwai.

After mastering the art, Ken Ming Kwai passed Pek Kwar down to his son, Ken Yung Kwai.

The Ken family was a recognized group of bodyguards utilizing the Pek Kwar system for protection. When Ken Yung Kwai's son came of age, he passed on the Pek Kwar style as well. His name was Ken Tak Hoi.

Summary

Pek Kwar kung fu is based on arm-swinging movements. It is extremely similar to Choy Li Fut kung fu. Though Pek Kwar is taught as part of Monkey kung fu, it has nothing in common with the art.

Chapter Five

The Weapons of Pek Kwar

The Weapons of

Pek Kwar
Kung Fu

The beauty of Pek Kwar kung fu is in its weaponry. It's not that the weapons used in the art are special or unique, in fact, they are less than a handful of the most common kung fu weapons. However, what makes the weaponry exciting is how it's used.

Unfortunately, it is not clear which member of the Pek Kwar lineage added weaponry to the art, but it is evident how much time and emphasis was placed in its creation.

Pek Kwar weaponry includes the double-edged sword or tai chi sword, long knife or curved sword and staff. The "choppers" which was mentioned in one article, was never part of the Pek Kwar art.

Double-edged/Broadsword/Tai Chi Sword

The most elegant weapon of the Pek Kwar kung fu art is the double-edged sword (also referred to as the Tai Chi or broad-sword). This is Grand Master Ken Tak Hoi's weapon of choice and one he excelled at extremely well. In fact, he was referred as the "Master Swordsman" for his accomplishments with this sword.

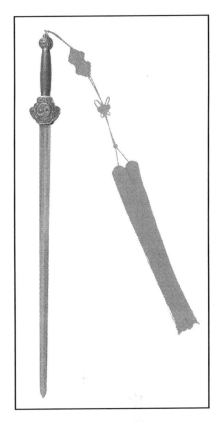

This is a beautiful form that is quite unique and it is also an extremely long form to remember. It has quick spurts of speed and a combination of thrusting and swinging.

The tassel is rarely used because the sword is swung so rapidly that the tails get tangled up quite easily.

The Pek Kwar sword uses a variety of balance postures and precision strikes. The sword should be strong and solid, not bendable like the Wu Shu sword. It is recommended that the student first purchase an $80 practice sword. Then, when he is comfortable enough, purchase a much more expensive and stylist sword to be used in performances and demonstrations.

The weight will be different so a practice transition will need to be mastered. When holding the sword in one hand, the length of the blade is measured near the ear areas.

The important thing about the sword is its deadly beauty.

The single-edged sword is a very fast moving weapon. Simple moves are easily learned but the Pek Kwar sword adds a little extra fluidity.

Single-edged Sword

This is sometimes called a knife or a form of the broadsword. The single-edged sword is slightly curved and only one side is sharpened. Next to the staff, it is the easier weapon to master.

The single-edged sword was the weapon of choice for the military in the early years because the basics could be learned in one day.

However, unlike most single-edged sword forms which incorporate slicing and cutting, the Pek Kwar form is very animated.

From jumping over the sword, spinning in the air and circular swinging, the sword moves at incredible speeds.

The two scarves at the end of the blade actually serve a purpose (as opposed to wiping the blood as noted in some texts). The scarves are used in a snapping motion to distract or even strike out at the opponent's face.

The size of the blade should be slightly shorter than the average sword. This shortened length will prove to help the practitioner in spinning and twirling the sword with room to spare.

Unlike many performance swords which are quite bendable, the Pek Kwar sword is more durable. However, the most important thing when learning the sword is perfecting the grip. It can become very easy for the sword to fly out of ones hands if the grip isn't secure, especially when spinning.

Special Hint: The best sword to purchase to do the Pek kwar sword with confidence is buying the double-sword. This looks like a single sword but it is actually two swords that are cut in half and fits into the same sheath.

The handle of the sword is actually cut in half so that one side is rounded and the other is flat. This odd shape allows the practitioner to grab the blade's handle more easily.

The Pek Kwar Staff

One of the strongest weapons of the Pek Kwar arsenal is the staff. It is powerful, strong and forceful. In many ways it is similar to the Hung Gar staff, but the Pek Kwar staff incorporates a large amount of spinning, twirling and rapid movement. Because of its twirling routines, the staff form requires the practitioner to have a very strong grip on the weapon.

Unfortunately, the Pek Kwar staff form has been often confused with one of the Monkey staff forms.

One of the reasons most Tai Shing Pek

Kwar students believe they are being taught a monkey form is because the staff being used by the instructor is made of silver (hence, the silver staff of the Monkey King). All monkey staff forms use the silver staff, Pek Kwar staff forms do not.

In addition, the teacher of the Pek kwar form is usually taught by a Monkey kung fu instructor and because he's so used to doing Monkey, he will un- knowingly add some little tidbits of Tai Shing postures and stances. It will naturally "look like Monkey" but in reality, it is not.

Pek Kwar staff "does" have some additional spinning and twirling in the form and to another kung fu stylist, it

Pek Kwar's staff form is very strong and powerful. It's filled with thrusts, stabs and pokes.

actually looks quite impressive. However, compared to a Monkey Staff form, it is quite simple.

Like other kung fu styles, the Pek Kwar staff form is very direct. It uses a large amount of thrusts, strikes with strong, powerful and low stances. Not monkey style low, but Southern style kung fu low.

There are no monkey stances or postures in this form, nor is there any such move as climbing the staff, which is actually a Wu Shu monkey movement. Some movements automatically identify a particular style of kung fu and climbing the staff is one of the most well-known pose that uniquely identifies it as the Wu Shu monkey.

The Pek Kwar staff is not silver, but primarily made of wood or bamboo and it's very hard and strong. The staff must be hard because it will be slammed and struck on the ground a number of times. The silver staff is reserved for the actual monkey staff form, so don't used a silver colored staff for Pek Kwar or any other martial art.

Summary

Pek Kwar weaponry is very different than the typical kung fu styles. Though it doesn't have free-swinging or twirling movements of the Monkey style, it does have unusual strikes, animated techniques and unique postures that make it very impressive.

Chapter Six

Grand Master Ken Tak Hoi

Grand Master
Ken Tak Hoi

Grand Master
Ken Tak Hoi

As one can see by the previous chapters of this book, the fate of the entire monkey system rested upon the shoulders of one individual, Grand Master Ken Tak Hoi. As Michael's instructor told him before moving away, "now you are responsible for passing on the art," therefore, the fate of the art today rests in Michael's hands as well (at least for America).

As far as anyone knows, Ken Tak Hoi was Grand Master Kou Sze's one and only student. Which meant that Grand Master Kou Sze passed on every detailed bit of information about the Monkey art he had earlier established. By default, keeping the Monkey alive was now up to Ken Tak Hoi alone.

This meant that Grand Master Ken Tak Hoi had to either create carefully written documentation of the Monkey art or just practice it continually until it was second nature; he choose the latter. That is why the publishing of this book is so important. Memorization may be the key to mastering the art, but it is the documentation that will keep it alive.

For many generations, the family of Ken Tak Hoi operated a highly successful escort and bodyguard service. They were proficient in hand-to-hand combat and quite skilled in weaponry and swordsmanship.

Ken Tak Hoi was a natural in the arts be-cause he was surrounded by kung fu masters all his life. Both his father and his grandfather were masters of the art of Pek Kwar kung fu. One of the weapons that fasci-nated Ken Tak Hoi the most was the straight sword also called the broad sword or Tai Chi sword.

He expanded his expertise of the sword by learning from other masters and monks. He became so proficient in the weapon that many referred to him as the "Master Swordsman."

After several years under his father's watch-ful eye, he felt his son was responsible enough and skilled enough to take on his first ap-pointment when he was only seventeen. His assign-ment was being a body guard at the royal palace.

Over the next three years, Ken Tak Hoi gained the respect of his

Here you see Grand Master Ken Tak Hoi, 2nd generation master of Monkey kung fu, demonstrating the Lost Monkey form.

clients and most importantly, his father. By the time he reached his 20's, his father helped him start his own armed escort and bodyguard service.

Ken Tak Hoi also took an interest in learning additional movements from a variety of other kung fu masters such as Sun Lu Tong, Ying Wen Bin and To Sum Ng. However, it was a suggestion from his grandfather, Ken Ming Kwai, that would change Ken Tak Hoi's life forever.

Ken Ming Kwai's best friend was another kung fu master by the name of Grand Master Kou Sze. Kou Sze was a Tei Tong practitioner and was sentenced to prison for eight years for killing a fellow villager. Through his years in solitary confinement with only a window looking out upon a community of playful monkeys, Kou Sze emerged with a new style of fighting called Monkey kung fu.

Because Kou Sze needed a protege to pass on his new art form, and Ken Tak Hoi was eager to learn from many different arts, putting them together seemed like a perfect match. Ken Ming Kwai made the arrangements and Ken Tak Hoi was introduced to his new master, Kou Sze.

Ken Tak Hoi was amazed by the abilities of his new teacher and how he performed the monkey art. It was something Ken Tak Hoi had never seen before. Ken Tak Hoi was additionally impressed in how powerful and strong Kou Sze's legs were. They moved like silk but were as powerful as iron. The local villagers also revered his strength and nicknamed him "Iron Legs."

After many years of learning (unfortunately, the timeframe of Kou Sze's instruction is not known), he charged his student to pass on the art.

As the 2nd generation master of Tai Shing and the 4th generation master of the art of Pek Kwar, Ken Tak Hoi began to spread both art forms. However, he openly taught the Pek Kwar art and reverently concealed the Monkey art. Only those who proved themselves as dedicated to the art would move on to learning the Monkey style.

Over his many years of teaching in both Mainland China and later Hong

Kong, Ken Tak Hoi taught a multitude of students in both arts. When he passed away, one of his advanced students, Chan Sau Chung, took over the Hong Kong school. Grand Master Chan Sau Chung is so gifted in the art that he currently carries the official title of "Monkey King." (Monkey kung fu keeps the tradition of recognizing only one living Grand Master of the style).

Grand Master Chan Sau Chung became the leading advocate for Monkey kung fu and was responsible for being the first to introduce the Monkey kung fu art to the American public through a variety of cultural exchanges with the United States and China in the mid and late 1970s.

Summary

Though Grand Master Kou Sze had only one student, Grand Master Ken Tak Hoi had a multitude of students. However, because the art is so secretive, many of the masters have chosen to keep the art within their own family clan. As a result, printing a family tree would be incomplete.

Chapter Seven

The History of
Tai Shing

The History of

Tai Shing

Unlike the amazing stories of ancient Shaolin in which the animal styles emerged from unique and fascinating circumstances, the history of Monkey kung fu is just the opposite. In fact, it is a story of bribery, treachery and murder.

photo courtesy of Kate James

Sun Wu Kong is one of the most famous characters in Chinese history. Crowned the Great Sage when he reached immortality, he became a hero in Chinese mythology. The Tai Shing art pays honor to this amazing Monkey King.

The art of Tai Shing is not an old style of kung fu, in reality, it is one of the youngest classical Chinese styles to date. Tracing back as early as the Ching Dynasty, the monkey style was developed around 1911 by a Northern Chinese fighter by the name of Kou Sze.

Kou Sze was arrested by the Chinese government for killing another individual. There are however, two stories on how Kou Sze committed the murder. The most common tale notes that Kou Sze had a short temper and as a result, got into a scuffle with a fellow villager and ended up killing him; with some stories saying the villager was evil, but some say he was not.

The second version reveals that Kou Sze was being forcibly dragged off to the military and he killed the officer in charge. Whatever the actual story was, Kou Sze committed murder and was sent to prison.

More often, the punishment for killing a fellow villager or a military officer would either be a death sentence or imprisonment for life. Fortunately for him, a rich and influential friend met with the judge to convince him to have leniency on Kou Sze. After a closed door negotiation and a hefty bribe, the judge reduced his sentence to eight short years. The judge decided that in order for Kou

The judge was bribed to reduce Kou Sze's sentence to only eight years.

Sze to suffer for his crime, he would require him to reside in solitary confinement for the full eight-year term.

For Kou Sze, it seemed like an eternity of wasting away in a tiny cell, but

Staring out his cell window day after day helped to break up the monotony.

little did he realize that he would emerge as a master of one of the most unique Chinese styles in history.

As a hot-headed fighter, Kou Sze was already well-trained in the martial arts. His primary choice of style was Great Earth kung fu, also called Tei Tong. Tei Tong kung fu is a form of art that is performed quite closely to the ground. It is a very strong and powerful style that naturally builds strength and stamina in the legs.

It contains a large variety of sweeps, unique rolling abilities and awkward leg kicking movements which requires balance, endurance and mobility in order to be effective.

To keep himself from going insane, Kou Sze practiced this art night and day and became quite skillful in a short period of time. His endurance level increased and his movements became lightning quick.

However, just practicing his kung fu day after day became quite tedious and boring. Luckily for Kou Sze, his little cell had one feature that he would spend a greater part of his solitary life, a window to the outside world.

The cell window did not face the village or even a road where he could see or talk to another human being, but instead, it faced a jungle with a forest of tall trees with hanging vines. There was also a large variety of creatures that quickly became his form of entertainment and an odd sense of companionship.

One day he was pleasantly surprised when a large colony of monkeys decided to relocate their home in the forest just outside his window. They came in all variety of shapes and sizes with plenty of young and energetic monkeys. For Kou Sze, it provided an opportunity to study the environment of monkeys up close and personal.

The Study of Monkeys

Hour after hour, he watched how the monkeys played and interacted with each other and in time, he was able to distinguish one monkey from another. He began to notice family groups, parent and child relationships and even sibling rivalry.

One item that apparently planted the early seeds of developing the monkey style was understanding the importance of the colony hierarchy. The leader of the clan and by far, the most impressive and strongest monkey of the group was the alpha monkey.

The alpha monkey is the ruler and reigning king of the monkeys. His word is law and everyone respects him. The alpha monkey is not always the oldest, but he is the strongest, the most cunning and the most experienced.

Scars cover his body showing his numerous and not always successful battles.

The alpha monkey also serves as the protector of the colony. When other, larger creatures would invade his domain, it was the alpha monkey that stood as the colony's line of defense. Obviously, the alpha monkey was sometimes quite small in comparison to much larger attackers, but it was the alpha monkey who would always lead a somewhat coordinated attack to drive the invader away.

For Kou Sze, it was the aggressive battles that drew the most interest in the monkeys

photo courtesy of Ben

A large colony of monkeys moved into the neighborhood. It gave Kou Sze a rare opportunity to study the habits of the monkeys.

behavior. He watched closely and studied how the monkeys interacted when being thrown into a stressful situation in which they needed to defend themselves, their family and the colony.

For monkeys, success was not always winning, but having enough wisdom to elude his attacker from certain death or to provide a window of opportunity in which his family members could escape.

Upon many occasions, there were a variety of challenges from within the monkey clan itself. Since the alpha monkey is the leader, his position was continually challenged by much younger and sometimes even stronger monkeys from his clan.

Though most of his contestants were from the young "teen group," it was the alpha monkey's wisdom that kept him alive and still head of the clan.

The fights were sometimes quick, sometimes long, but all had a definitive outcome - submission or death.

Defining the Monkey Characteristics

In addition to the fighting aspect, it was the characteristics of the monkeys that intrigued Kou Sze. In some fashion, each monkey was able to interact with their attackers applying their own unique personality.

The alpha monkey, who was obviously the stand-out with his strong presence and threatening abilities, was successfully able to defend himself, just as much as his opposite, a much smaller and weaker monkey.

The small monkey, which Kou Sze later referred to as the "Lost Monkey" was usually the youngest, most playful and a monkey that was always being somewhere he didn't belong. Being naturally curious, he would occasionally wander off the path and get left behind the pack and would become lost; hence

photo courtesy of Mario Prado

the Lost Monkey title.

As soon as the little monkey realized that he was alone and lost from its family, it would panic. Frightened and scared, the lost monkey would run feverishly through the jungle looking for a fellow monkey that would lead him to his family. As darkness came, the lost monkey become so anxious that he would jump at every sound and his eyes bulged in fright as he would wildly scamper through the jungle looking for the way home.

Like an injured fish frantically splashing in the sea attracting sharks from miles away, it was the lost monkey's scampering that attracted larger creatures looking for an easy meal. After all, how hard could it be to capture such a light snack as a frightened, little monkey in the jungle all by itself.

However, to Kou Sze's surprise, when the lost monkey was attacked, its traits of confusion and quickness served to his advantage rather than a disadvantage. Instead of becoming frozen in fright, the lost monkey would run, jump and leap wildly from one direction to the other. Striking out at the attacker with his limited reach, the lost monkey would move quick enough to remain out of the larger creature's reach.

He would jump on his attackers' back as hard as he could, then leap away so quickly the beast couldn't get a fix on his position. The monkey was so elusive, the aggressor couldn't get a handle on him. Again and again, the monkey

Until recently, Grand Master Michael Matsuda was one of the last two individuals to master the entire monkey system in America. However, by the time this book will be printed, Grand Master Matsuda's student, C.J. Martinez, will have mastered the entire monkey art, thereby becoming the first 7th Generation Master of the art. Grand Master Michael Matsuda is shown here demonstrating one of the movements from the monkey forms. Though each monkey characteristic is different, they still share about 80 percent of the same moves.

would attack and run quickly away. It would be impossible for such a small monkey to go one-on-one with the beast, so his alternative was a quick in-and-out form of offense.

As the small monkey would scamper from one direction to the next, the larger creature found that this lost little creature was taking too much of his time and eating him as a snack was no longer worth his energy.

For the small monkey, his victory was not a death blow or crushing strike to his enemy, but one of elusiveness and escape. He was unable to get fully away from his attacker, but he was quick enough to get out of the way.

Kou Sze felt this monkey's own unique traits helped it to survive. Though he was small and looked like an easy prey, his movements of panic and confusion made him elusive and untouchable. As a result, Kou Sze began to examine other monkeys and record how they were able to draw on their own personality to survive in the jungle.

The Mind of the Monkey

The transition of movements from monkey to man was an easy task for Kou Sze. Because he was already a very accomplished practitioner of the Tei Tong style, which was already low to the ground, converting it to a monkey art wasn't too difficult. Since monkeys have arms and standing positions like a human, he was able to easily adapt these techniques into a more human art.

The challenge however, was how to effectively adjust his approach to fighting. Rather than the usual punch and block routine, Kou Sze had to develop

In practicing Monkey kung fu, one must consider their own body-type. For example, if the are small or lightweight, the movements of the lost monkey may fit them better. Or if the person is larger or stronger, the stone monkey may be a better fit.

a strike and elude approach. In other words, he had to re-learn what he had been practicing for decades.

Kou Sze had to alter his face-to-face form of fighting with a battle of cunning wisdom, quickness and precision. In addition, he had to apply a specific per-sonality to a specific way of attacking.

For a monkey, the chances for sur-vival against a larger

photo courtesy of Mario Prado

beast are quite small, so his timing and severity of his attack, if he is able, must be dynamic. It was no longer an defensive/offensive reaction, but an offensive survival mode.

This meant that if a window of opportunity opened in which the monkey could strike his attacker in a vulnerable position, he had to make his strike as severe as possible because he may never get such an opportunity again.

After watching the various types of monkey characteristics and examining how each reacted in many life-threatening situations, Kou Sze decided to create five different fighting methods based on five distinct monkey types. They included:

The Lost Monkey
The Stone Monkey
The Tall Monkey
The Drunk Monkey
The Wooden Monkey

Because each monkey type was completely different from each other, Kou Sze created five extremely long forms which allowed him to easily separate each monkey style. Obviously, all five monkeys shared many of the same movements such as walking, rolling and jumping, but each separate personality had to be reflected in the forms. He had to create the mind of the monkey for each monkey type.

The Lost Monkey

The lost monkey, as pointed out earlier, was the smallest of the group, the one who got separated from the pack and appeared to be lost.

In order to incorporate Tei Tong successfully with the movements of the lost monkey, Kou Sze had to establish a unique form of monkey walking. Somehow it had to resemble a monkey, yet a human had to be able to perform it.

Because each one of the five forms represented a monkey, the same walking movement had to be incorporated for each. However, because this particular primate is smaller than the

photo courtesy of Mario Prado

Like all monkey forms, the Lost Monkey is very long. In fact, they are the length of three regular kung fu forms. All five monkeys share many of the same movements such as walking, rolling, jumping and more. However, it is the Lost Monkey that is more animated than the others. As a result, this is the only form that will ever win in forms competition because though the others are still monkey, they don't have the same fast pace, facial movements and nervousness as the others. The Lost Monkey is not a difficult form to learn and if taught correctly, can be mastered in a short period of time.

rest, it would have to remain extremely low the ground; more so than the others.

For Kou Sze, this would be the defining characteristic of the monkey style. All kicks, techniques and rolling patterns would be delivered from a low position. This entailed creating a different method of training including an emphasis on balance. Such common movements as kicking would have to be altered to fit the

photo courtesy of Karen Gonzalez

The Lost Monkey is performed quickly and very low the ground. It's the best for performances.

monkey style, and they must still be just as effective.

In addition, timing for a high kick versus the timing for an extremely low kick had to be re-evaluated.

Since the monkey was lost, the practitioner would also need to adapt this persona. He also had to mimic the expressions of a frightened monkey as he looked anxiously from side to side. The gestures had to be quick, extended, then pulled back into a small, close to body position. This was a different monkey than the rest because of his vulnerable characteristic, and the form had to reflect that.

Since the lost monkey form would be the foundation in which the following four monkey forms would be based on, Kou Sze spent additional time examining the little monkey's posture; trying to imitate his movements, stances and motions. In addition to his mannerisms, the lost monkey would occasionally scream and yell at different points of the attack. However, it would be pointless for a lost monkey practitioner to scream at the top of his lungs throughout the entire form. The monkey stylist would run out of breath very quickly and screaming all the time would dishonor the form.

To make an appropriate adjustment, screams are used quite sparingly and placed at different points of the form as a type of deception.

The lost monkey form had to be a burst of energy and power because it was both advancing and retreating. Kou Sze created spaces of fixed positioning. In other words, the lost monkey didn't have to go through the complete form in just one motion. He felt it would be more effective to divide the form into small, short bursting segments but still remain as one long form.

Quick, fixed pauses would serve two purposes: A) Provide a position for the monkey to change its direction and; B) Allow the practitioner to catch a slight breath and prepare them for the next segment.

The lost monkey form, as with all the other monkey forms, is designed for any individual to learn, no matter the body size or type. However, some practi-

photo courtesy of Marc Lawrence

tioners who are slightly smaller may be more comfortable using the lost monkey techniques as opposed to a tall person feeling more familiar with long, swinging type techniques as in the tall monkey.

The Stone Monkey

Developing the Stone Monkey form was probably the easiest of the five. Patterned off the abilities and characteristics of the Alpha Monkey, stone is the most defined monkey; strong, powerful, hard, large, dominating, unapproachable,

The Stone Monkey is the most powerful of the five monkey forms. Using the elbow, knee and more, the Stone is brutal to its opponent.

The Stone Monkey is better designed for someone who is strong and solid.

photo courtesy of Mario Prado

daring and in one sense, slightly more predict-able. One always knew where he stood when challenging the Stone.

As noted earlier, Stone is undoubtedly the leader, the dictator and boss, but most of all, he is the protector of the clan. He is the first line of attack and the last line of defense.

Though it seemed this monkey would have a more face-to-face approach against his enemy, we cannot forget it is still a monkey. To a tiger or a panther, it is still a small, fragile monkey that would be a nice and tasty morsel.

Like the lost monkey, the stone monkey form had to maneuver in a low stance, and have a quick attack mode like a monkey. However, being the alpha monkey, its movements had to be much stronger, powerful and bone-breaking.

Since the Stone couldn't move as fast as the lost monkey, delivering a blow to its opponent must be executed with such an impact that it would cause severe damage to its attacker, thus giving Stone additional time to get away. However, for Stone, escaping from its attacker is not always its goal. For example, if Stone severely injures its opponent and the opportunity presents itself, stone will remain with the fallen foe in order to deliver a series of fatal blows.

In addition to its menacing presence, the stone monkey includes a larger arsenal of attacking methods such as elbow strikes and punches, knee strikes and double fisted techniques. These additional movements require the practitioner to have a strong, more solid body that must be able to absorb a more brutal regime.

Unlike his peers, the stone monkey relies more on its knuckles for walking and maneuvering rather than its palms. Therefore, building a little callus on the knuckles comes with the territory. In addition, wrist strengthening is highly recommended to support many of the movements that involve balancing with one arm using a knuckle position on the ground.

The stone monkey form is Michael's favorite because it focuses primarily on strength and power. This fits his body type more than the other monkey forms. The stone form is the easiest to learn for most martial arts practitioners because the transition is not as severe. Training is more familiar and the stances for the Stone are both high and low so adjustments can be easily made.

Of all the five monkey types, the stone monkey is also by far the most effective. It uses aggression, combined with power and sheer strength, to defeat its opponent. Though it must still maneuver as other monkeys do, lightning fast speed is not required to elude its attacker.

The Tall Monkey

As Kou Sze examined the movements and mannerisms of both the strong, the small and other petite monkeys, another type of monkey that Kou Sze felt stood out from the group was actually the tallest monkey of the bunch. Hence the type, "tall monkey" resulted.

The majority of the monkeys in the colony were all quite small in stature, even the alpha monkey measured fairly close in height to its peers. However, the one trait that made

photo courtesy of Karen Gonzalez

The Tall Monkey in many ways is similar to Choy Li Fut. Obviously, it includes the monkey rolling, jumping and walking, but it also includes a huge variety of arm-swinging motions. Being the tallest of the bunch, the Tall Monkey has the longest reach and takes advantage of that extra distance. This is the easiest of the five monkey forms to perform.

this monkey different was not only its height, but the length of his arms and legs which allowed him to reach further and leap higher.

And it was that extended reach of the taller monkey that inspired Kou Sze to create the tall monkey form.

The tall monkey's height was also an advantage when trying to escape from an opponent, he could always reach to the higher branches to pull himself out of harm's way.

The lost monkey was obviously the quickest of the bunch, but the tall monkey managed to keep up with

photo courtesy of Marc Lawrence

The Tall Monkey includes a variety of low and high stances so most people find it easier on the body.

bigger and longer strides.

When it came to fighting, his extra reach provided the monkey a little more breathing room to strike the opponent from a further position, which enabled him to escape a little more quicker.

Using careful analysis, Kou Sze decided to utilize the tall monkey's resourcefulness and incorporate a series a long arm, circular hand movements that no other monkey included. Stances would be slightly taller than the other monkeys, with the ability to shrink down to a low position. Kicks would be slightly higher but it would recoil quickly. The swings would be hard and powerful, but like all monkeys, Tall must be elusive and mobile.

Training for the tall monkey requires a great deal of fluidity, and more distance in the jumping and leaping modes. After all, it is a larger target so getting away must be through distance leaping and jumping.

One major requirement for tall monkey training is the ability to incorporate proper breathing into the form. While this applies to all monkeys, it is more crucial in the Tall. The tall monkey is the only form that consists of a large amount of circular arm striking and in order to strike properly, the entire arm including the fist must relax through the swing until the last moment of impact. With requiring mobility and fluidity, proper breathing allows the practitioner to create that type of moment.

Because of its reach, the tall monkey is mostly a better fit for taller practitioners. The tall monkey is similar in many ways to Choy Li Fut kung fu because of its long arm strikes, but because of its mobility, the similarity ends there.

The Drunken Monkey

Perhaps the monkey with the most unorthodox style of maneuvering and fighting is the drunken monkey.

There is no doubt that monkeys are curious creatures; so curious in fact that it often gets them into trouble.

One area of curiosity that amused Kou Sze was when the monkeys would wander into the nearby village and make a pest of themselves and annoy the food vendors. The monkeys would steal everything they could get their little hands on; fruit, poultry, but one item they especially loved was grabbing bottles of alcohol.

Not waiting until they returned back to the colony, the monkeys would drink their tasty bottles of wine all along the way. Over a short period of time, they found themselves quite disoriented and because their little bodies couldn't hold the liquor, they would be falling all over the place.

Like the small monkey who seemed like easy prey when lost, the drunk monkey must have appeared as the easiest thing on the menu.

Though the other monkeys had their own style of protection, Kou Sze couldn't imagine how an intoxicated monkey could ever defend itself let alone maneuver itself from being eaten. But much to his amazement, the drunk monkey became a formidable opponent.

As the drunk monkey was being attacked, its swaying and unbalanced

The Drunken Monkey is one of the most difficult to learn. Not because of the movements, but because the practitioner must manuever in a broken and off-balance rhythm.

photo courtesy of Mario Prado

photo courtesy of Marc Lawrence

The Drunken Monkey must have looked like an easy prey for a beast of any size. Afterall, what can be more delightful than trapping and eating a disoriented monkey. However, since the monkey was already able to defend himself sober, he would still carries some of those techinques over when he was not.

The Drunken Monkey should be very low to the ground. This will make easier on the body to fall from a lower position.

motions caused it to fall back awkwardly thus avoiding the larger creatures lunges.

Its constant weaving, off-balance pattern and broken rhythm made it a more difficult target to attack.

Sober, the monkey was quite skilled, but even though it was intoxicated, it was still able to slightly defend itself.

The movements were still the same, but the approach was more broken and unpredictable in its timing.

Combining Tei Tong with drunken monkey was not an easy task. The drunken monkey's agility was extremely different from the usual drunken man forms that many people have seen sometime in their life. Drunken man employs a huge variety of back flexibility moves and cuplike drinking actions. But monkeys don't use cups and they don't stretch their backs in the same way that humans do.

To match the movements of a drunk monkey, Kou Sze used off-balanced movements of swaying and leaning in different directions. Though the monkey seems to be drunk, it must still be in control of its fighting movements.

In order to take advantage of its many falls, Kou Sze added off-balance falling kicks, side rolling and multidirectional strikes. Instead of the usual blocking movements, the arms moved in a semicircular position sometimes hitting the opponent or sometimes just balancing itself.

The kicks and punches still had to be hard and effective, and using proper breathing and balance allows the practitioner to focus his energy to the final moment of impact. The practitioner must have the appearance of being intoxicated, but must execute with power and strength yet still be elusive. The drunken monkey artist must learn to avoid a punch with an off-balance maneuver, then counterattack with a kick or punch with speed and accuracy.

This is the most difficult monkey to learn correctly because of its awkwardness and approach. At times, it leaves the body in a position of vulnerability but the practitioner must be able to move quickly within seconds.

Drunken monkey like lost monkey, is very low to the ground. As a result, performing a drunk monkey fall is much easier on the body as opposed to falling from a much higher position.

photo courtesy of Mario Prado

Facial expressions also play a role in convincing the opponent that the monkey is intoxicated. Kou Sze noticed that even though the monkey was disoriented, it didn't seem as frightened when being attacked. Also, there was no need for screaming because the drunk monkey didn't really care as much as he would if he were sober.

Though any bodytype can fit the drunken monkey's style, it is more suited for a thinner individual who can provide less of a target for the attacker.

The Wooden Monkey

The last and final of the five monkeys is the wooden monkey form. Now, unlike its title, the wooden monkey should have been called the bamboo reed monkey because one of the two key factors of this form is its mobility. Obviously, this does not pattern a monkey made of wood, but it does pattern a monkey that is quick, bendable and can explode quickly when attacked.

The wooden monkey is very similar in many ways to the lost monkey. Both are scared, both are nervous and both move with great speed and maneuverability. However, the distinction between the two is the method in which they interact with their attacker.

Another key factor and perhaps the best adjective that stands out most when explaining the characteristic of the wooden monkey is "sneaky." Unlike the lost monkey, who would run away from its attacker by jumping and distancing itself away, the wooden monkey's goal is to lure in the opponent to chase it then when almost caught, Wooden would quickly turn the tables by quickly spinning around and leap out toward its enemy with an aggressive attack that would surprise and ultimately subdue him.

In other words, Wooden would act like he's fearful and running for his life, but all the time he was planning for just the right moment. When the attacker thought it was going to have a nice desert, the monkey turned and took advantage of the situation. In brief, it was a setup.

Kou Sze observed that the wooden monkey performed the same types of movements when playing with its fellow monkeys as well, but obviously not as aggressive.

Now because the wooden was still small, it had to take into account the reach of the attacker. Should the attacker get its hands on the little wooden monkey, that would be it, therefore, wooden had to plan its movements to move quick enough to stay just barely out of reach.

Another item that set wooden monkey apart from the rest was its unique walking pattern. Like the drunken monkey, walking is multi-directional, which allows the wooden monkey to change directions quickly.

Because of its unpredictable leg movements, learning the wooden monkey is very demanding the legs. Like the lost monkey, it is also very low to the ground. There is a lot of low running, hopping and in the air twisting. It does share the same rolls as the others, but because of its deceptive mentality, it must be extremely quick in order to be effective.

The wooden monkey must always be in control of its movements and still be able to run in a setup pattern.

photo courtesy of Karen Gonzalez

Timing is everything for this monkey. It must be able to act like its running away from the battle, but turn the tables around so quickly that it must shock its opponent into a moment of confusion. And in that moment is when the wooden monkey conquers its attacker.

However, its movements, such as the rolling, must be measured carefully, otherwise the monkey could be in jeopardy if his landing is not far enough away.

Therefore, the wooden monkey must study the reach of its attacker so that it can adjust its movements properly.

photo courtesy of Karen Gonzalez

The best word to describe the Wooden Monkey is "sneaky," because it will entice the opponent to follow him, but suddenly flip around to attack.

Emerging as Monkey Kung Fu

Passing the time

away day after day, year after year seemed unbearable, but spending his time enjoying and learning from the monkeys made it somehow pleasurable.

It took some time, which Kou Sze had a lot of, but he was able to take the low postures of Tei Tong kung fu and add the most unique characteristics of the five monkeys and create an unorthodox fighting style of kung fu he called Monkey kung fu.

Based on grabbing, falling, rolling and low maneuvering, Monkey kung fu became a style that was hard to combat against because of its impracticability.

The five forms; lost, stone, drunken, wooden and tall would be the trademark of the monkey style and all those who mastered them would truly be a

photo courtesy of Angela Martinez

Monkey kung fu is a very, very difficult art. One member of the military came to the class and said the workout was way tougher than he had ever experienced. These are the latest crop of Monkey students that continue to endure. From left to right, Mitch Norris, Sifu Drew Smith, Grand Master Michael Matsuda, Master C.J. Martinez and Sifu Joshua Freedman.

powerful and unyielding force.

To honor the great Monkey King from the famous Chinese folklore "Journey to the West," he called the art Tai Shing, meaning "the Great Sage."

Summary

The basic formula is to match an individual's body type and personality with a particular monkey. In other words, a taller person would be better suited to learning just the Tall Monkey. A stronger person would only be taught the Stone Monkey. Unfortunately, no one except Master Matsuda has lasted long enough to reach this level.

This is not a hard art to learn, just a hard art to practice.

Chapter Eight

The Weapons of Tai Shing

The Weapons of
Tai Shing

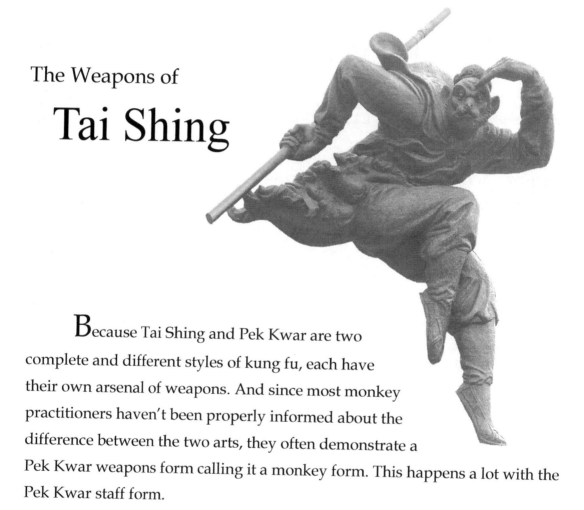

Because Tai Shing and Pek Kwar are two complete and different styles of kung fu, each have their own arsenal of weapons. And since most monkey practitioners haven't been properly informed about the difference between the two arts, they often demonstrate a Pek Kwar weapons form calling it a monkey form. This happens a lot with the Pek Kwar staff form.

There are two weapons associated with Tai Shing: The monkey staff and the monkey ring. Though other publications have listed additional weapons for the monkey, they are in actuality Pek Kwar weapons, not Tai Shing.

The staff is the primary weapon of Sun Wu Kong, The Monkey King. Tai Shing uses a silver staff to show honor. However, sometimes the Monkey King is pictured with a gold staff or sometimes silver with gold ends. The illustration above is from the book "The Monkey King: A Superhero Tale of China," retold from "The Journey to the West" by Aaron Shepard (Author).

photo courtesy of Aaron Shepard

The Monkey Staff

Without a doubt, the most famous and well-known weapon used by the monkey practitioner is the staff. Sun Wu Kong from the Chinese folklore "Journey to the West," brought fame to the weapon by selecting a magical silver staff which he could sometimes tuck under his ear to quickly retrieve it to use it in battle. Nearly every statue, drawing or painting of Sun Wu Kung shows him posing with his magical staff.

The staff is called the "father of weapons" by all martial arts stylists. It is the most basic weapon and one of the most powerful of weapons. The staff is strong and quite difficult to block against.

Most styles embrace a large amount of staff blocking, striking, thrusting and more. Though the monkey staff does include these movements, its approach is completely different.

Grand Master Kou Sze, founder of the monkey style, decided to include one choice of weapon for the monkey; the staff, because it was similar to what the monkey was already used to.

For example, in order to extend his reach to acquire a fruit from a nearby tree, the monkey selected a long twig or broken branch to knock the fruit down. To retrieve insects for a quick snack, the monkey would stick a long twig into the insects den and pull out a stickful of tiny morsels. Choosing a weapon such as a sword for the monkey wouldn't have made any sense.

Since the forest was loaded with twigs and branches, the monkeys would often pick up a stick and begin playing with

photo courtesy of Angela Martinez

Sifu Joshua Freedman and Master C.J. Martinez stop for a pose in learning the Monkey staff form. The Monkey staff uses the silver staff as shown here. The Pek Kwar staff, which is not taught at Grand Master Matsuda's class, uses a wooden or bambo staff. Matsuda's students are the only individuals in America who know both Monkey staff forms.

it. Putting it over his shoulder, the monkey would walk around the whole colony striking and hitting every object he could find.

On some odd occasions, when another animal attacked the colony, the monkey would get the stick and use it to defend itself or continually poke at the beast to drive it away.

Like a human, the monkey used the staff in a variety of situations, and because the monkey had movements similar to a man, Kou Sze adapted these movements into a more human approach.

The Application

The staff, like the monkey handform itself, is comprised of quick and twirling movements. Resting on the shoulder like a monkey, the practitioner must be able to jump, land and even roll while keeping the staff secure in one hand.

Unlike the linear approach to staff attacking, monkey stylists add multidirectional strikes and like the lost monkey, it must disappear quickly. However, like the wooden monkey, it must turnabout to deliver a powerful blow to its pursuer.

The monkey staff, like the tall monkey, must include proper breathing to move freely and flowing. But like the stone monkey, it must strike with force and strength.

Working with the Staff

Staff training is very different in the Monkey art. Though it does have the basic strikes and blows, it also adds a high element of quick spinning and twirling and if not practiced correctly, could send the staff sailing from your hands. In addition, spinning the staff also provides a unique tool for strengthening the muscles in both the grip and arm movements.

To prepare for staff training, it is important to follow a basic process that will help the practitioner considerably in becoming an expert in this weapon.

Selecting your Weapon

The first thing is
As adjustments for monkey
and balance, the same rule
rect staff that will fit your
finding the exact height of

To measure the
individuals bodytype,
staff on the floor. Stand
with feet about six
balance the staff with
locate your ear and the
should be between the
earlobe to the top of the
height on your staff.
height of the staff for

It's very impor-
the appropriate length,
ner begins spinning
behind them, if the
or scrape the
ground and could
cause injury to the hand.

selecting the appropriate staff.
training is based on body type
applies to choosing the cor-
body. This includes
the staff.
staff correctly for an
place one tip of the
completely straight
inches apart and
one hand. Now,
height of the staff
bottom of your
ear. Now, mark that
That is the actual
you.
tant that the staff height be
because when the practitio-
and twirling in front and
staff is too long, it will strike

Here, Monkey kung fu senior student
Joshua Freedman poses with the staff.

photo courtesy of Angela Martinez

The Monkey Staffs

One of the most unique advantages of practicing the Monkey staff is that it automatically develops a strong, vice-like grip. When monkeys fight, one of the first things they do is grab their opponent tightly. Twirling the staff will help tremendously in improving ones grip. However, in order to begin, it is recommended that the monkey practitioner train with three different types of staffs.

The most important thing in the world is to keep the staff from flying out of your hands. Therefore, having a strong grip begins with staff twirling. It is best to start with a heavy, large staff and work your way to the lighter, silver staff.

The Larger Staff

The first staff purchased should be a wooden staff that is significantly thick; about two inches or more, depending upon the person's hand size. Using a thick staff will force the practitioner to grab the staff strongly when twirling. Since the staff is quite heavy, it will require the monkey stylist to use muscles in their arm that have seldom been used.

The larger staff will build the arm muscles properly and prevent the weapon from flying out of the hand when doing a monkey staff form.

A steel or metal staff of the same thickness would also work fine, it just needs to be heavy.

The Medium Staff

The second staff should be purchased about three months later or when the practitioner feels they have conquered the larger staff without dropping it. The medium staff should be about an inch or so in thickness and because this staff is much lighter, it will be easier to maneuver.

A bamboo staff will work just fine but it is recommended that the silver staff be purchased in order to get used to the smoothness of the weapon. Semi-heavy aluminum will work perfect as the student adjusts to the different feel of the staff.

The monkey's silver staff was said to have magical powers. It could extend to the heavens and shrink so small that it could be hidden behind the monkeys ear. Today, Monkey kung fu practitioners use the lightweight silver staff to give honor to Sun Wu Kong, the Monkey King of the Chinese folklore.

The Final Staff

If the monkey student is able to twirl the staff with great speed in a variety of maneuvers without dropping it, then it is time to move onto the final staff, the silver staff.

A silver staff is used to give honor to the Monkey King of the Chinese folklore, Sun Wu Kong. The staff should be extremely light to enable the stylist to twirl the weapon with excessive speed. Practicing with the lighter staff will need some adjustment, but once mastered, it will look like the wind.

Acquiring the Staff

Locating the monkey silver staff is not as difficult as most people think. One thing to keep in mind is that the silver staff is used for demonstrations or photographs. Because it is so lightweight, a dent will immediately appear if it strikes an object.

Acquiring the silver staff has been a secret from the general public. However, this secret is about to be revealed.

Like a treasure map, the secret of where to purchase the magical silver staff is from the shower curtain section of your local hardware store. Because the staff is so "extremely" lightweight, one competitor used to hide the staff after he performed, but allowed others to examine the more heavier staff thereafter. The picture above is the famous Newhall Hardware store in Santa Clarita owned by Victor Feany.

The silver staff should be made of polished, chrome material. The more shiny the better. It should be extremely lightweight so that it can be spun a lighting fast speeds. The ends of the staff must be covered because an open edge can cause injury if the staff flys into the audience and strikes someone.

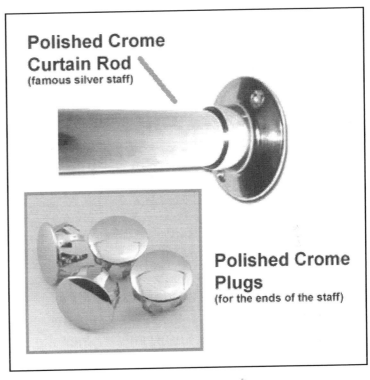

Polished Crome Curtain Rod
(famous silver staff)

Polished Crome Plugs
(for the ends of the staff)

Now please follow these directions closely: 1) Go to your car; 2) Drive down the street until you find your local hardware store; 3) Locate the bath and toilet section; 4) Then look for the shower curtain section and there you will find a stack filled with dozens of the famous monkey silver staffs.

Yes, that's correct. The actual secret to the silver monkey staff is that it is a shower curtain rod. The lighter the shower curtain rod, the faster the spinning will be. Please be sure to polish or buff the staff so that it gives an additional shine as it spins.

Be aware, that there are several different weight levels in the shower curtain rod area. The goal is to have the staff spinning fast and blazing so getting the lightest staff is a priority.

Never, ever use a staff that is open on both ends. If you drop the staff when spinning, and you will, the open end can cut a circle mark on the floor and if someone is struck by the staff, the open end can cause serious injury.

To seal the end of the staff, just purchase some polished chrome plugs. The plugs have teeth to grip the inner part of the staff but use some super glue as well to secure a tight fit.

Special Note

There are several things to be aware of when using the silver staff. Because both Wu Shu and Tai Shing use the same weapon, it is easy to get them confused.

Climbing the staff: There is a move that is quite famous in the monkey staff form. This is when the monkey stylist will plant one end of the staff on the ground and climb it like a ladder and balance themselves at the top while looking around. It's a very comical move and amazing to perform. However, this move is only performed by Wu Shu monkey and the Chinese Opera monkey.

This move is part of their art and to accomplish it is a difficult feat. However, there is "no such thing" as climbing the staff in actual Tai Shing Monkey.

Standing on the staff is NOT a Tai Shing move, but a Wu Shu or Opera Monkey pose.

The staff is the practitioner's primary weapon and using the staff weapon to display a "performance monkey move"

As one can see, the opponent needs only to knock off the bottom of the staff and the monkey would be vulnerable.

puts the weapon in jeopardy of bending and breaking. It also puts the monkey practitioner in an extremely vulnerable position of falling or being struck. So don't ever stand on your staff!!!!!

The Monkey Ring

There's a lot of controversy surrounding the Monkey Ring because Grand Master Kou Sze never created a monkey ring form. In reality, having the monkey ring doesn't make much sense. There were obviously plenty of branches the monkey could use, which would account for a staff form, but it would be safe to assume large monkey rings weren't spread out all over the forest.

No one really knows how the monkey ring became part of the monkey's arsenal and that's usually why it is seldom referenced. Nevertheless, we'll address it.

The monkey ring is about 24 inches wide and slightly thinner than the staff. However, like the staff it is also silver in color.

Some say that the monkey ring occurred when Sun Wu Kong, the Monkey King, might have bent his staff into a circle to create a different type of weapon.

Master Matsuda poses with a make-shift monkey ring. He didn't have one so he had to re-create it. However, the monkey ring can be purchased at ValleyMartialArts.com..

photo courtesy of Angela Martinez

(Ok, just a thought.)

The ring is big enough to be worn over one shoulder and under the other arm; much like carrying a knapsack. This allows the practitioner to walk and even fight until the ring is needed.

In order to be effective, the ring must be very durable and strong. Some use an iron ring coated with silver.

The ring is used primarily with both hands and used for blocking other weapons, however, it can easily break a bone if used to block a punch or kick. Because the striking is limited by its size, the blows are usually quick and short.

The inner part of the ring can also be used to trap other weapons such as a spear, staff or even a sword. If quick enough, the opponent's kick can be trapped and twisting the ring can cause quite a bit of damage to the leg.

Another method of using the ring is as a leg sweeping device. Holding the ring in one hand, the ring is swung at the opponents legs. Unfortunately, there are no forms for the ring, only techniques.

Summary

The monkey staff form is the only weapon required to learn in the monkey art. It is extremely different than any other staff form in Chinese kung fu. Loaded with multi-directional spinning, unusual swinging patterns and a multitude of high and low movements, it is one of the most celebrated weapons of kung fu. There are two monkey staff forms in the art.

Chapter Nine

Flexibility

photo courtesy of Mario Prado

Learning Monkey

Flexibility

Over the last several years, the topic of flexibility and East Indian arts such as yoga have brought an ire of confusion in Monkey kung fu training. Amazing, contortionist feats may impress judges at a tournament, but such movements have never been part of Tai Shing kung fu.

Movements such as placing a foot around the head, laying on their back with their head through the legs can only cause injury to the body should a muscle be pulled, but more importantly, these postures leave the monkey practitioner in a very vulnerable position should he be attacked or threatened.

When Monkey style kung fu was originally designed by Grand Master

Kou Sze, his goal was to combine the movements of the monkey along with his Tei Tong techniques in order to form a highly combative fighting art form. He felt that if he could take the best qualities from the different monkeys and apply them successfully together, a powerful and highly effective fighting system would emerge. One cannot believe he would spend eight years of his life in order to create an art to impress a crowd of onlookers.

It is obvious that monkeys are uniquely flexible. They can do unusual and mind-boggling feats such as grabbing vines with their feet and be completely outstretched. However, just because a monkey can put his face to his butt doesn't mean it should be added to the system.

Because Grand Master Kou Sze wanted monkey as a unique form of martial arts fighting, he had to incorporate movements that would be to the monkey's advantage. Therefore, an appropriate posture must allow the monkey to either defend itself or to strike out against an opponent.

Simply put, Monkey kung fu does not include extreme flexibility in any of its five monkey forms. It would be wiser if a student devoted their time mastering the monkey art rather than wasting valuable years of practice attempting to excite a tournament judge with flashy yoga positions.

Flexibility Training

In order to be comfortable practicing and fighting in Monkey kung fu, there is a certain amount of flexibility that must be adhered to. In any form of martial art, stretching the legs can provide an easier path to reaching a higher target with a little less pressure. In addition, doing some flexibility movements during the warm-up will help the body adapt to the routine much quicker and avoid injury.

However, flexibility in the monkey system focuses on two vital areas that will help improve the overall effectiveness of the art. They include:

Ankle Flexibility

Mobility

Ankle Flexibility

One of the more unique aspects of Chinese kung fu are the stances. Held relatively low to the ground, it builds strength in the legs. Stances, like that of the horse stance, is the most difficult because of the intensity on the lower half of the body.

Monkey kung fu stances, on the other hand, are very different to say the least. Because the monkey tries to maintain a much lower stance throughout the entire form, the practitioner must employ a different set of rules altogether.

Now, the monkey stances in itself

photo courtesy of Angela Martinez

Here you can see the areas that require flexibility training; in the ankles and the back of the heels. Please notice the height of the heels to the floor. Continual practice will help stretch this area.

are not as difficult as it may seem. The goal is to do the stance correctly, that is the key. Monkey stances, which include the monkey walks, begin with first learning how to stretch the ankles.

It has often been thought that training in monkey will damage the knees because of the low stances. Yes, it will -- if learned and practiced incorrectly.

If the monkey stances and maneuvers are done improperly, the weight of the body will have an impact on the knees. This will result in tension on the knee, pain and even irreversible damage.

However, in order to perform the maneuvers the right way, spend a great deal of time stretching the front of the ankles and back of the heels. It is the ankle flexibility that will allow the body to sink down into an extremely low position with no stress on the knees.

Obviously, when first starting to learn monkey some discomfort will be initially felt at the knees. However, as the ankles begin to stretch, the knee pressure will be reduced dramatically until it can't be felt at all. (You will, however, feel aches and pains in the leg muscles as well, but that's another story.)

There are two areas to keep in mind when attempting to achieve ankle flexibility and proper stances. The first area of concern is the back. There should be a real effort to keep the back straight. The back will tend to lean slightly forward, but attempt to keep it upright as much as possible.

photo courtesy of Mario Prado

Mobility is required to manuever from one area to the next very quickly. This is extensively for both the Wooden and Lost Monkey forms.

Keeping the back straight will effect the second area of concern which is the placement of the heels.

A ultimate goal is to stretch the ankles until both feet fully lay flat and parallel to the floor. This will help to build leg strength and add stability to your stances. But, don't worry if you never get your heels on the ground, most people don't. As long as you can balance yourself properly, your stance is just fine.

Mobility

Monkeys tend to move very quickly in a variety of situations. From playing with their friends, frolicking through the jungle, running after a tiny morsel or just running in a circle, monkeys are known for their speed and agility.

The second key to monkey flexibility is mobility. By keeping the body fluid, the monkey practitioner will develop an ability to move quickly from one direction to the other.

For example, the wooden monkey is known for his sneakiness. That sneakiness is made possible by maneuvering from one direction to the other very quickly.

If the body is stiff and rigid, moving quickly will be awkward and slow. The body must be agile and able to sway from one area to another with ease and ankle flexibility and mobility will help significantly with mobility.

Summary

The most important part of Monkey kung fu is being able to maneuver in a very low stance. The kicking, punching and rolling are all based on low pos-tures. Therefore, creating flexibility in the legs must be developed. Concentrating on stretching the ankles will not only accomplish this task, but it will make practicing monkey a lot easier for years to come.

Chapter Ten

Chi Kung

photo courtesy of Karen Gonzalez

The Cultivation of
Chi Kung

Learning to breathe properly is applicable for every style of martial arts. Chi, also call Chi Kung or Ki, allows the body to move more freely and transfer the power within to an external strike or kick.

There are many excellent books and DVDs on the market that can provide a detailed program in learning to cultivate one's Chi.

As far as Monkey kung fu is concerned, the same techniques apply, however, we must take into account the location of the body. Since most monkey postures are extremely low, it sometimes takes an extra effort to concentrate on getting the stance correctly, making sure one is able to maneuver properly and still remember to breathe from within to cultivate the chi and exhale to release it.

Though each of the five monkeys utilize chi kung, two of the monkey forms require an additional amount of attention; the Tall Monkey and the Drunk Monkey.

Performing the Tall Monkey requires and extensive amount of circular arm movement. Most practitioners tend to swing their arms with power and force. Though this may be effective if the target is struck, it limits the capability of the stylist.

For Tall, the arm movements must be free-flowing and quick. This will enable the strikes to seemingly come out of nowhere and make additional strikes, not just one.

Having a strong fist and tightened arm will make the technique slow and awkward. The arm, including the fist must be loose and the momentum must "flow like water". The moment of impact is when the fist tightens and the energy is released.

To improve one's mobility in the arms, appropriate breathing must be applied. The energy must be built up from the abdomen and released through the arms.

There are a variety of breathing exercises for this particular form which will be explained in books or DVDs to come.

For the Drunken Monkey, the breathing is similar but released throughout the entire form. Unlike the Tall Monkey, which uses the chi in its arm swinging movements, the Drunk Monkey uses the chi to keep its balance, move in an awkward rhythm yet still produce effective kicks and punches.

Drunk Monkey must be mobile and elusive, yet unassuming. It must release its power effectively yet maintain its character.

Granted, this is a difficult concept to understand, but when performing these particular monkey forms, it will be easier to comprehend.

Summary

Learning the mechanics of the art such as punching and kicking are essential, but incorporating appropriate breathing methods will help develop the art to its full potential. Monkey kung fu does not employ its own Chi Kung movements, but it does utilize Chinese breathing methods that were developed many centuries ago.

Chapter Eleven

Learning the Art

Learning the Art of

Monkey

photo courtesy of Marc Lawrence

Monkey kung fu: The lineage is so short you can literally count the names of those who have completely mastered the style. It is an art that is misunderstood but an art that is very respected.

However, "Monkey kung fu is not for everyone." This is a statement that Master Matsuda has continued to make over the last 30 years. It is a statement that has been repeated by every monkey stylist since. (Now you know where that phrase originally came from.)

The reason why there are only a handful of Monkey masters is not be-

photo courtesy of Karen Gonzalez

Because Monkey kung fu is so difficult on the legs, thighs and knees, nearly all the students will drop out after the very first lesson.

cause the art is reserved for only certain individuals, its just that 90 percent of those who attempt to learn Monkey kung fu will drop out within the first few months.

This is a very, very demanding art. The size and weight of the individual does not matter, but it is the endurance level and the ability to practice while in extremely low positions.

This is what most people hate about this art, the low walking, standing and rolling. The body doesn't have to be in top fitness shape, but it must be able to maneuver quickly and efficiently.

In order to practice this art, one must already have a substantial background in another martial arts style. Monkey kung fu does not lend itself to learning basic movements, such as how to execute front kicks, side kicks, punches, etc. This is a highly advanced art form and in order to learn the full aspect of the art, one must have the basic tools already perfected before taking a step into the monkey world.

Training

Training in the art after the first day will be the hardest. If taught correctly, the new student will begin by learning the monkey walks. From there, they will continue with the low monkey maneuvers, the angular movements, the rolling movements to the simple kicking from a low horse position. The legs of the practitioner will be sore for at least one full week from just one hour of training.

This is not because the new student is out of shape. It's just that different muscles are used and strengthened and that's what makes it so tough.

For every monkey, walking is essential and running is extremely critical. To emulate a small creature, training must be reactive, quick and sudden. Conditioning the legs by doing monkey walking will improve the mobility for such active movements.

Remember, first the knees and thighs will hurt a bit, but when the pressure on the knees are removed, only the muscles will be sore. This is where correct teaching comes in; if the knees continue to be strained after the first couple of months, too much pressure is being placed on the knee and this should be immediately corrected.

Preparing

Stretching is of course essential before doing any type of exercise, getting the legs warmed up first is the key to preventing pulling or straining a muscle. Cardio, warm-up exercises are essential prior to any low monkey training. Incorporating a jump rope routine will help the body to not only get warmed up, but will help your endurance tremendously.

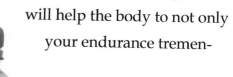

One very vital sug- gestion when practicing Monkey kung fu is to get into the habit of drinking plenty of water throughout the whole day prior to working out in the Monkey art. Since the stylist will be continually moving from high to low positions in an instant, the lack of water may make the head slightly dizzy and fainting can occur. Drinking plenty of water prior to training will help reduce this risk.

The Floor

When Grand Master Matsuda first began studying Hung Gar kung fu at the Hollywood school, the floor was made of hard, smooth concrete. Despite wearing rubber-soled shoes, the smoothness caused the students legs to slide out, which made it extremely difficult to hold a proper horse stance. However, by using the toes to grab the floor from inside the shoes, it reduced sliding to a minimum.

But, because the training was so hard, the students would sweat so much that a small pool of salty water in front of them would form which caused all the students to slip and fall.

This is the actual floor from the Hollywood Hung Gar school. Here, Michael is doing a cat stance. Notice the smoothness of the floor. It is not tile, it is very hard concrete. The inset photograph shows the unyielding floor he learned Monkey kung fu on.

When Matsuda began learning Monkey kung fu, he studied in the driveway of his friend's house which was made of hard, crusty concrete that cars drove across daily.

Eventually, when his Monkey training expanded, they trained at one of the student's garage, which also had the same familiar smooth concrete.

Though Grand Master Matsuda trained in the old method of rolling on hard concrete, a thin carpet was later brought in to assist the new students in learning the art. Today, it is highly recommended that a rubber turf or mat be used for learning the art.

Rolling improperly on cement will quickly cause a bruise on the shoulder and Master Matsuda had plenty of them in the beginning. The shoulder must be tucked in perfectly and the roll must go across the whole back rather than a single spot which will cause injury.

photo courtesy of Mike Swain

Though a concrete will force the student to perform the rolls correctly, it's better to start with some type of foam flooring.

Laying down a long tape as a guideline will help the student to roll or walk straight and correctly. Obviously, rolling on concrete will let the student know immediately if the roll was performed correctly, but it's better to start on a rubber-type mat so that adjustments can easily be made and bruising will be kept to a minimum.

The Uniform

Kung fu styles are known for their amazing uniforms. For example, Mantis kung fu has both black and white uniforms with ties underneath both arms. Hung Gar uniforms are usually black satin that have a wrap around sash in the center and serve to hold up the pants. If not wrapped correctly or never ironed to stretch out the sash, the pants could easily fall to the ground. (It has happened.)

The art of Monkey kung fu does not have an official uniform, per se. Grand Master Ken Tak Hoi demonstrated many times in his socks and regular clothes.

However, in order to give honor to kung fu itself, traditional black, satin uniforms have become the norm for the Monkey art. Before searching in the local garment stores and purchasing a few yards of black satin to create the uniform, please be aware that there are several types of black satin. Picking the wrong one will result in having to iron the uniform before every workout because some materials wrinkle so easily. Another satin to avoid is one with a more denser material. This will prevent the uniform from breathing and cause a "green house" effect, meaning the student will begin sweating the moment the uniform is put on.

A crepe-type satin is recommended rather than the extremely shiny material which wrinkles quite easily. Crepe satin is still quite shiny, but if examined closely, the material will look very similar to crepe paper. Unlike the more common satin, the crepe material is quite difficult to wrinkle. Crepe material also breathes much better than the traditional satin and it is easier to work with. Plus it flows a lot better.

All satins will eventually fade into a dark purple coloring. However, the crepe satin will take a significantly longer time to get to this point.

The Top

Notably, the most obvious part of the monkey uniform is the top. Traditionally, most kung fu uniforms have the higher, upright collar and that applies to monkey as well.

Sleeves should always be long so that it can easily blend in with the rest of the uniform. By blending the uniform with longer sleeves, the monkey strikes will be more deceptive. For practicing, the sleeves can always be rolled up a bit.

The end of the sleeves should have a cuff-type finish, usually fixed by two snap buttons.

The most crucial part of the top is the buttons. There are many types of Chinese buttons including the frog buttons, the knot and loop buttons, etc. To keep the uniforms consistent, the interlooping buttons are highly recommended.

Interloop buttons are two rows of loops on each side of the top. To affix, one begins at the top and goes downward as one loop slips into the other. There are approximately 26 loops on each side but that can vary.

To secure the top, the last button is a knot and the last loop just simply

photo courtesy of Michael Matsuda

Long Sleeves
(rolled up when needed)

Interloop Shirt Ties
(not buttons, but loops)

Baggy Shirt
(for movement)

Baggy Pants
(for movement)

Tie String
(hanging out because
it looks cool)

Shoes
(black with no heels, boots
or slips will fall off)

attaches to it. There is also a knot at the very top so that it can be buttoned for photographs.

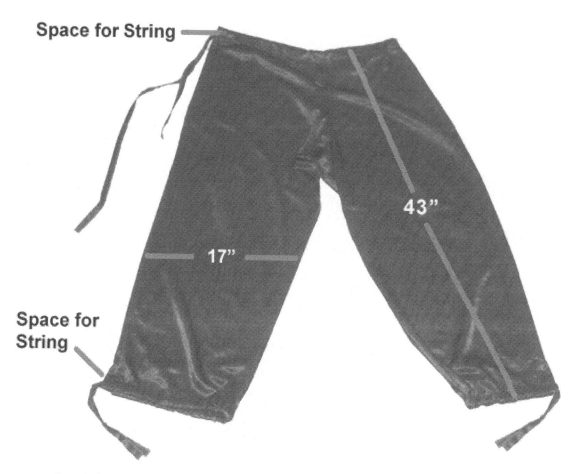

Space for String

43"

17"

Space for
String

Special Note: Looping the uniform will become quite tedious after a few workouts. Therefore, it is suggested that the top five loops be left unlooped so that the top can be slipped on like a t-shirt.

The Pants

First off, the pants are a one-size-fits-all. It doesn't matter how tall or big one may be, the pants are all the same size (if you are over seven feet, adjustments will obviously need to be made).

The width of the pants should be about two legs wide, 17 inches actually. The larger leg width allows the body to move in odd type positions and serve as a tool of deception. The pants should also match the same fabric as the top.

Do not use elastic for the bottom of the pants because it will not allow the pants to move as freely. As the student makes an unusual turn, elastic will twist the pants and reveal the next move.

In addition, the bottom of the legs should have a tie feature. Use double knots when tying the leg because if a single knot is used, the quick movements in Monkey will cause it to unravel.

Because the ties are made of satin, they will have a tendency to fall back into the pant loop. In order to restring, it is recommended that the student attach a safety pin somewhere on the uniform which will help tremendously when trying to restring any of the ties.

Create a long, horizontal loop or tunnel at the top which will allow the practitioner to insert a long strand to tie the pants together. The strand should be made of the same material. In many cases, the strand will be seen when doing monkey rolls. Loop the strand through the pants just once and tie the excess to the right side.

Because the pant legs are 43 inches, there may be an excess in the leg length. To adjust, simply tie the bottom loop slightly higher from the ankle on the inside so the pants don't drag.

The Shoes

Another element of the uniform is the shoes. Nearly every kung fu style uses shoes and Monkey is no different. Though shoes come in a variety of types, black has been the tradition.

Long Boots

Wu Shu Shoes

Short Boots

The shoes should be flat and heel-less. The best type of shoe for monkey style is the long boot. The long boot fits high up the leg which hides the sock or skin. In addition, it also looks very classy. Unfortunately, the long boot is extremely difficult to find.

Short boots are very popular to wear as well, however, for the monkey art which moves quickly from one direction to the next, the short boots tend to slip off very easily. They look great for photographs, but are a pain to wear when working out.

Wu Shu shoes are Grand Master Matsuda's choice of shoes for training in

This is one of the official Monkey kung fu shirts worn in both China and America. The writing reads "Tai Shing Pek Kwar men." Men means style. It is suggested that the practitioner wear a black shirt under the uniform because all the monkey forms require intense rolling and the bare back will be exposed.

photo courtesy of Angela Martinez

monkey. They are quite similar to American tennis shoes but without the heels. These shoes can usually be found in a Chinatown or through a kung fu supply store. Wu Shu shoes only comes in sizes under 11 inches.

Again, this is the individual's choice. Because there will be a lot of jumping and rolling, the student must select something that is more comfortable on the feet.

T-Shirts

A black t-shirt should always be worn underneath the uniform top because since the student will be rolling, their bare back will continually be displayed for all to see. A t-shirt will prevent that.

Grand Master Matsuda has produced a number of official Tai Shing Pek Kwar shirts available to his students.

This is one of the many Chinese opera outfits worn by an actor portraying Sun Wu Kong. It is used by both the Wu Shu and Opera monkey styles.

The Monkey King outfit from the Chinese opera is a very intricate, detailed and quite spectacular costume to wear. However, a Tai Shing practitioner should never wear this costume to represent or perform the monkey art.

The Wu Shu monkey and Tai Shing monkey are completely different arts and should be honored accordingly.

Learning Pek Kwar

As noted, Grand Master Kou Sze created the complete Monkey art form. It was the combination of Tei Tong and his addition of monkey characteristics. Grand Master Kou Sze never taught Pek Kwar kung fu because he never knew or practiced the art.

Learning from Grand Master Matsuda, you will begin day one in learning the Monkey art (Tai Shing) and won't practice a single move in Pek Kwar.

Grand Master Matsuda devoted 30 years of his life to learning everything about the complete Monkey system. From its history, its methodology to its fighting and weaponry. Now, because he does not teach Pek Kwar, mastering Monkey will take a shorter period of time as opposed to three decades.

Monkey Screaming

Each of the five different monkey types have their own unique characteristic. Some are scared, some are powerful, some are sneaky but all are effective.

Monkey screaming is primarily used for the Lost Monkey form. Since the lost monkey got separated from the rest of the group, he's naturally scared, excited and very fearful. Every noise and disturbance around him makes him anxious and very jumpy.

When he is attacked, he jumps and screams and makes all kinds of unusual sounds.

For the lost monkey form, the screams and yells are placed in certain locations as a form of deception. The yells will take the attention away from the monkey's attacks. It's a very effective tool for the monkey.

However, screams should never be used throughout the entire form. If one screams the whole time, the air of deception is quickly lost.

In addition, since the forms are quite low the practitioner will easily run out of breath and stamina so the movements must be paced correctly. If one screams all over the place, additional energy that is needed to complete the form

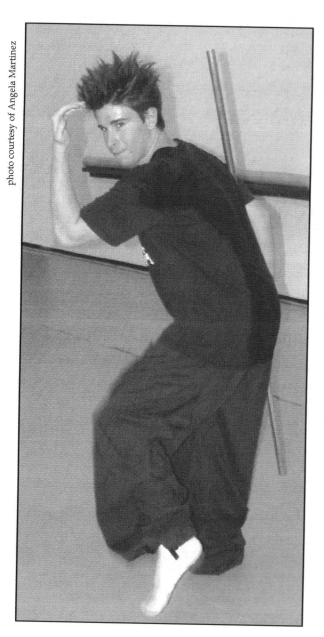

photo courtesy of Angela Martinez

will be used up and the practitio-ner will end up being out of breath when the form is complete.

Therefore, please use the screams as they were meant, as a deception, not to attract everyone's attention to a performance.

The Belt System

Traditional kung fu systems in China have never used a formal belt system. A sash was used primarily to hold up their pants.

Kung fu schools were based on a level system: new students would start in the "beginner level" class, continuing students would jump to the "intermediate level" class and senior students would practice in the "advanced level" class.

Master C.J. Martinez demonstrates a move from the Monkey staff form.

The proper name given to the senior students is "Si Hing". The appropriate term for the teacher is "Sifu", which actually means father because the art of kung fu was designed to be a family group. Si Hing means older brother.

photo personally given to Michael

Grand Master Chan Sau Chung is the only individual who can rightly hold the official title of "Monkey King."

Because most martial arts schools in America have adapted to Western customs, belt or sash level rankings have become normal practice.

Therefore, the United States Tai Shing Pek Kwar Association has decided to incorporate belt levels if the school desires to use them.

Remember, Monkey kung fu is an advanced form of martial art. This means all students must already have an extensive background in kicking, punching, etc. Therefore, advancement in the art may not take as long as some other styles.

Senior students are those who have completed one of the five monkey forms. They are considered green belts.

First degree black belts are awarded to those who have completed at least three of the five monkey forms. This would be an instructor level position with the title of Sifu.

The title of master is reserved for those who have completely mastered the entire monkey system, including all five
forms as well as the monkey staff.
This would eliminate the need
for creating specific degrees such
as 2nd degree black, 3rd degree
black, etc.

Official Tai Shing Pek Kwar certificate awarded to Sifu C.J. Martinez.

Certification

The United States Tai Shing Pek Kwar Association was designed to keep
the art of Monkey kung fu in America as pure and true to tradition as possible.
Because the art is limited to only a handful of individuals, the association was
formed to honor Grand Master Kou Sze, the founder of the system, and to pass
on the art to the next generation.

Most martial arts styles are hundreds, even thousands of years old. Many
have remained true to their original form while others have either watered-down
the art or added their own movements into the art. This causes a lot of confusion
to students who are trying to learn the traditional art form.

The U.S. Tai Shing Pek Kwar Association was formed in 1999 to properly
ensure that students are learning the Monkey art as close to the original as pos-

sible so that the art can be passed on correctly.

The association will ensure that any inappropriate movements or made-up techniques are removed from the actual teaching (such as Yoga, religion, Taoism, extreme flexibility, etc.).

By becoming certified as a student in the association, it will also make sure that those who plan to teach the art will have proper teacher certification and listed as an authentic Monkey kung fu school.

Certified schools will also be listed for others to access.

Summary

This chapter has provided some little tidbits of information that will make learning Monkey kung fu more enjoyable. Grand Master Matsuda feels it is important that a form of consistency be developed for the movements, uniforms, certificates and more.

Chapter Twelve

Monkey Fighting

The Art of

Monkey Fighting

The Result

When it all comes down to it, it's the end result that really matters. While lightning fast, colorful or silky performance may impress a tournament crowd, it's the overall effectiveness of the techniques that immediately tell if you are doing the art correctly. Fancy, twirling kicks may look amazing, but if a kick is unable to do damage to an attacker, then what's the point.

At the turn of the century when Kou Sze spent nearly a decade in solitary confinement, he devised a form of fighting that he felt was extremely powerful

photo courtesy of Angela Martinez

Monkey kung fu was originally designed as a brutal and powerful fighting art. Here, Grand Master Michael Matsuda quickly traps his opponent (C.J. Martinez), violently pulls him to the ground and prepares to deliver a fatal blow. This is part of the Stone Monkey form.

yet very unorthodox. To put it simply, Grand Master Kou Sze's goal was to create a kung fu style with an approach that it would be so unusual that would not only be difficult to fight against, but the end result would cause the opponent to suffer great pain and injury.

In order to accomplish this, Kou Sze had to change, even abandon his prior concept of fighting entirely. Though he had become familiar with each of the monkey's behavior in similar, life threatening situations, his next task was to examine the method of the approach.

It was obvious that a face-to-face encounter with a much larger opponent would be suicide for the little monkey and

Kou Sze had to establish a method in which each monkey's personality would be used to his advantage.

since most creatures were twice his size, a different and more challenging approach was required. The typical punch blocking had to be completely revamped to fit the monkey stylist.

Since an attack on a monkey was fighting for his life, the monkey's mentality must be in a survival mode, in other words, it had to fight hard, brutally hard with great cunningness in order to escape with its life.

To put it in basic terms, every battle for the monkey is a life-threatening situation with the odds drastically in the enemy's favor, however, despite its dilemma, the monkey must somehow still survive.

Examining the Advantages of the Monkey

There are, however, many attributes that monkeys already have that make them formidable fighters. The following are a few examples that Kou Sze was able to take advantage of:

Strength:

Despite their small stature, one of the most powerful attributes of the monkey is the strength of their grip. Over many years of grabbing and pulling vines or just hanging from a tree branch, helped enable the monkey to acquire a vice-like grip.

As a result, Kou Sze made grabbing and pulling an integral part of the art. Rather than just blocking a punch or strike, the monkey would grab the arm like grabbing a tree limb. Instead of pulling its body to the tree, the monkey practitioner would grab and pull the opponent toward him or toward the floor in a variety of directions.

Speed:

Perhaps the most visible asset to the monkey's arsenal is their speed. They are fast, extremely fast and for the most part, that's exactly what keeps them alive. The smaller monkey will lead in this category, but all monkeys have their own form of quickness. Remember, monkeys have to maintain a distance from its attacker so being unreachable is one of the keys to its survival.

Monkeys, as in the Lost and Wooden, uses their speed to avoid their attacker while monkeys like Stone and Tall uses their own speed to attack, then retreat.

Mobility:

Mobility is the unique ability to move quickly and easily from one position or direction to another. For example, the monkey walk can proceed in one direction and within seconds, reposition itself, turn at an angle and go in a completely different direction.

By adding some movements of flexibility, it allows the body to be more mobile. Flexibility does not mean performing ultra stretching moves that put oneself in a vulnerable position of attack; this is not Monkey kung fu.

Wooden monkey requires the most freedom of mobility in order to perform quick, multi-directional changes.

Unpredictability

Another unique advantage when fighting is using a monkey's version of unpredictability. Though the Wooden monkey is the most unpredictable, all monkeys share a measure of unpredictability.

Each monkey practitioner must make certain adjustments to take advantage of their skill level or body type. For example, some stylists favor kicking over the punching, as a

photo courtesy of Angela Martinez

Because the monkey is usually much smaller than his attacker, he must look for vulnerable positions that would impair him. Here, Master C.J. Martinez strikes the upper rib of senior student Joshua Freedman. Notice how the monkey grabs the opponents arm, twisting it in order to control the enemy, then notices a vulnerable area of the body and strikes.

result, they will have a stronger tendency to use a more comfortable move against an enemy such as kick as opposed to a practiced punch resolution. Therefore, the monkey fighting habits of the one monkey practitioner may differ significantly than another. Thereby, making the form of combat even more unpredictable.

The Fighting Concept

Breaking down the concept of Monkey kung fu fighting is very difficult to explain. It's not just different, it's extremely different. Now, for the majority of those reading this book, one would safely say that the average martial artist is quite familiar with the fighting concept of one-to-one competition, where one opponent faces off with another.

With monkey fighting, the concept of defense/offense has to be altered to

photo courtesy of Angela Martinez

The Stone Monkey uses his elbows, knees and other areas of his body to cause severe pain to his opponent. Of the five monkey forms, the Stone Monkey is by far the most powerful of the bunch. Here 6th Generation Monkey Grand Master Michael Matsuda delivers and elbow blow to student Mitch Norris.

understand how the monkey mind works.

Perhaps, one of the most basic and best examples that will explain the monkey fighting concept is when a much larger creature, like a tiger, invades the colony of monkeys looking for a mid-afternoon snack. The tiger is huge, powerful, fearless and hungry. Now, it would be impossible for a monkey to stand toe-to-toe with the tiger, even suicidal. Even the stone monkey, with all his strength and power, wouldn't stand a chance.

This is where Kou Sze had to completely tear down and re-examine the approach. When a human stands toe-to-toe with another, each has some margin of chance over the other. Depending upon experience and skill, the end result is uncertain. In other words, both have a chance of being victorious. But as pointed out earlier, for the monkey this is not the case; the monkey must find a way to escape death.

Kou Sze found that he was able to analyze the monkey's mind and determine specific factors that changed the outcome and allowed the monkey to survive basically unharmed.

The Approach

To throw one's idea about confrontation out the window is a hard concept to swallow. Learning how to block and counter has proven to be effective for thousands upon thousands of years, but Kou Sze had to do exactly that; dump all his prior knowledge of confrontation.

Intimidation, fearlessness, survival of the strong all pay a contributing role in taking the upper hand and conquering one's enemy.

However, this concept only applies when there is at least a chance that one opponent can dominate the other.

With a beast such as a tiger, the monkey does not have even a millionth of a chance. But, somehow, the tigers are driven away hungry and monkeys still exist today. So, the question is, how do the monkeys survive?

The Methodology

This is where the explanation of monkey fighting gets very tricky.

As stated earlier, a monkey is being confronted by a larger beast, he will lose. Now, stay with me. When you, as an opponent

go head-to-head, you will lose. Now, don't stop reading.

The little monkey knows its limitations, knows he cannot defeat his opponent in a face-to-face encounter, so he must have an alternative plan for survival. The alternative is what makes monkey fighting unique.

As a human practitioner, it is your goal to look for an alternative form of confronting the enemy rather than going toe-to-toe. In many circumstances, you, as a human can easily defeat your opponent in a more typical fashion, but that's not what Monkey kung fu is about.

Examining the Approach

Now, let's examine both the approach and methodology together in the following example:

<u>Example One:</u>

Once again, a hungry, ferocious tiger follows a monkey to find its lair. The monkey sees the tiger approaching and yells out to the rest of the colony that a huge beast is about to enter their home and attempt to devour them.

As the tiger leaps into their small village, it is the rigid stone monkey he first sees as he lands. Crawling slowly toward his prey, Stone quickly jumps out of reach as the tiger advances forward and pursues.

And, just when you think the tiger is about to catch stone, another monkey gallops out of the bushes just inches behind the tiger. He is so fast and close that he grazes the tiger which throws him completely off-guard.

As the tiger quickly turns to look for this new assailant, another monkey runs by and strikes the tiger and runs back into the jungle.

For the monkey, he is striking the tiger with all his might, but for the tiger, it is just a touch, even an annoyance.

All of a sudden, two monkeys attack at different angles and one even uses a short stick to make a poke at the tiger as he goes by.

The screams of the surrounding monkeys get louder as other monkeys join in on the attack by throwing rocks and sticks from the trees above.

For the monkeys, the tiger is a threat to their lives and they are brutally attempting to cause great bodily harm to the beast. For the tiger, their attempts at painful application is like a pin-sticking annoyance, but it's a continual annoyance.

In time, the tiger decides that these tiny creatures are not worthy of his efforts, so he moves on. Hence, the monkeys are victorious over this large beast causing him to leave hungry.

Understanding the Example

This example points out the monkey's cunningness in avoiding a more treacherous opponent, knowing they didn't stand a chance one-to-one, the monkey utilized a play of action in attacking the tiger from different angles, in a sense, finding his vulnerable and blind spots.

The monkeys choose not to be on the defense, but to attack its opponent. Which brings this example to its final point, the monkey knows if it defends itself, there is a 100 percent chance he will not be successful and in this circumstance, failure means loss of life, therefore, he chooses the best and most effective option, attack.

Example Two:

If the monkey is attacked by an opponent which may be closer in size and stature, the methodology remains the same.

The little monkey again refrains from the face-to-face confrontation even though the enemy may be an easier opponent than the tiger, the monkey

photo courtesy of Angela Martinez

Senior student Josh Freedman locks C.J. Martinez on the neck and kicks behind the legs to knock him down while choking him.

leaves nothing for chance.

Like fighting with the tiger, the monkey must look for an opening by keeping a safe distance from the enemies reach and moving in different angles. When it sees an opening, it attacks with all power and might.

photo courtesy of Mario Prado

Though forms may be the primary area of learning in kung fu, it must be sprinkled with tons of powerful training.

Here, Grand Master Matsuda is demonstrating a move using the more formal uniform.

Keep in mind the monkey mentality of the first example. The life/death confrontation is still the same. The human monkey practitioner must do everything possible to injure the opponent, so it must attack.

The key to the attack is to utilize powerful and strong blows to a vulnerable area. (We'll get into this part in the next publication.)

When fighting, there will only be a small window for attack and the practitioner must look carefully for that window which he will use to cause great bodily pain.

Remember, as a monkey, you are the prey, therefore the practitioner has the option of continuing to hop around in different angles to find a window of opportunity to open.

To put it simply, when a monkey practitioner is confronted, he must continue to maneuver out of harm's way. All the while looking for an opening in his opponent's defenses so that he can attack.

The Alternate Goal

For the monkeys, victory is not always the same. Gathering together and driving away a ferocious and powerful attacker such as the tiger from their home is the victory, even if they didn't kill the tiger, they just annoyed it away. Nevertheless, a victory was attained.

If the monkey was cornered, but yet escaped with his life, that would be the victory as well.

The monkey stylist doesn't always have to defeat his opponent until he is

photo courtesy of Angela Martinez

Grand Master Matsuda trains students who already have a background in the martial arts. Because Monkey is an advanced art, students should already have mastered how to punch, kick, etc. Since Matsuda is only teaching the Tai Shing art and not Pek Kwar, his students will be in the advanced mode from day one. This also means it will take less time to master all five forms and the complete system. Here Si Dai Mitch Norris, Master C.J. Martinez, Sifu Josh Freedman and Sifu Drew Smith perform a move from the Tall Monkey form.

completely incapacitated, however, his goal is to brutally injure the opponent by striking a vital point so that he is in so much pain that he cannot return to strike or chase the monkey.

Summary

Monkey kung fu fighting is fierce. It is a "no surrender attitude" with an attack mentality of causing brutal pain and injury. In addition, the monkey must also create a door of escape to survive.

Obviously, there is a great deal more to the actual monkey fighting, but this book is primarily on history and tradition. Fighting techniques will be available in future books and DVDs.

Chapter Thirteen

The Legend of Sun Wu Kong

Mask of the Monkey King used in the Chinese Opera.

The Chinese Folklore:
Journey to the West

The Legend of Sun Wu Kong

The name of Sun Wu Kong has been synonymous with the Chinese art of Monkey kung fu. It is always mentioned with great respect and honor.

The term "Monkey King," given to the highest ranking individual in the Tai Shing art, is worn as a tribute to Sun Wu Kong.

Grand Master Chan Sau Chung is the only currently living monkey master who can properly wear this title today. The monkey staff itself, is finished with chrome, silver or gold to pay deepest respect to the legend of Sun Wu Kong.

Because of these and other continual references to the Monkey King, it is important that every Monkey kung fu practitioner become familiar with the ancient Chinese folklore of "Journey to the West."

"Journey" is perhaps the most beloved and traditional folklore in Chinese historical literature. It is a classical novel which was originally published

photo courtesy of the Disney Channel

Kim Possible was a cartoon series aired on the Disney Channel in 2002. Creators of the cartoon are Mark McCorkle and Bob Schooley. An Emmy Award winning animation series, Kim Possible includes a character called Monkey Fist, an expert in Tai Shing Pek Kwar.

in the 1590s during the Ming Dynasty. The true author of the story remains anonymous, however, the closest name attached to this piece is a writer named Wu Chen-en.

Because of its originality, the story is performed consistently throughout Chinese operas, puppet theaters, films and animation. Adaptations of the character of the Monkey King can be found today in a variety of cartoons and animations.

Kim Possible, an emmy-award winning animation on the Disney channel includes an arch enemy named "Monkey Fist," and who happens to be an expert in the Chinese art of Tai Shing Pek Kwar.

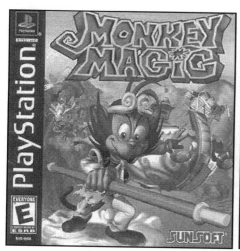

Interactive games are a billion dollar industry throughout the world. Filled with martial arts figures and battles, the Monkey King is no exception.

Here you find Playstation's "Monkey Magic" and Wii's "The Monkey King" games.

In 2008, Chinese martial arts actors Jackie Chan and Jet Li portray a different version of the Monkey King in the "Forbidden Kingdom." Jet Li starred as the great Sun Wu Kong.

In a recent television movie "The Lost Empire," Russell Wong also took on the challenging role of the Monkey King. Interactive and video game producers Playstation, X-box and Wii have all thrown their hat into the ring by creating a series of games featuring the adventures of the Monkey King.

Even the world famous Rose Parade in Pasadena has including a variety of floats featuring the Chinese folklore.

The Journey

The novel of "Journey" is a fictionalized account of a story that revolves around a Buddhist monk and his pilgrimage to India in order to retrieve reli-

Illustration of Journey To The West. The painting is a decoration on the Long Corridor in the Summer Palace in Beijing, China.

gious texts which are called the "sutras," and bring them back to China. The monk must make his long journey to the West accompanied by three protectors. The story is not only a quest, but it is an adventure, a fantasy, a personal search and even a political satire. Journey is based on a true story of the actual monk Xuan Zang and his real journey from China to India and back to China again in 629 AD. Since then, the account of his story has evolved into an amazing fantasy adventure.

In the folklore, the Buddhist monk is named Tripitaka (aka Xuan Zung) and his three protectors are made of two other monks named Sha Seng (aka

Sandy), Zhu Ba Jie (aka Pigsy) with Sun Wu Kong (aka the Monkey King). These three characters have agreed to help escort the monk Tripitaka on his journey as an atonement for their past sins. The most memorable part of the story revolves around the lives of the main characters, but it primarily focuses on the story behind the creation of the Monkey King, in his rise and fall of power.

Because this story is centuries old, many artists and storytellers have made certain adjustments or additions to the adventure, but the overall interpretation is still the same.

Tripitaka

Tripitaka (Xuan Zang) is the primary monk assigned to set off to India to retrieve the religious scriptures and bring them back to China. Though considered the leader of the group, he is human and has many human frailties. For one thing, he is easily deceived by

The monk Tripitaka assembles a legion of misfits to escort him from China to India and back to China.

others, especially the Monkey King, and he possesses no skills in combat so he is also unable to defend himself and must depend completely on his escorts.

Nevertheless, it is his duty to prove himself as a mentor to the others and show his trustworthiness by successfully bringing back the scriptures while avoiding demons along the way. It has been written in some texts that if a demon eats the monk, he will gain immortality.

Pigsy

Pigsy (Zhu Ba Jie) was once an immortal Grand Admiral of 800,000 soldiers and Marshal of the heavenly river. But during a Peach Banquet in celebration of the gods, he drank too much and flirted boldly with Chang'e, the beautiful moon

goddess, resulting in his punishment of being sent down into the mortal world. He was supposed to be reborn as a human, but ended up in the womb of a sow due to an error at the reincarnation wheel, which gave Zhu Ba-jie the appearance of a half-pig, half-man.

As part of a team of misfits, the great Ba-jie was once a great admiral and marshal. However, because of his drinking, he was reborn on Earth as a half-man, half-pig and was nicknamed, Pigsy.

Sandy

Sandy (Sha Seng) was once the Curtain Raising General whose duty was to guard and escort the imperial chariot in the Hall of Miraculous Mist. However, he was exiled to the mortal world and made to look like a monster because he accidentally smashed a crystal goblet

Sandy was exiled to the mortal world and made to look like a monster. Living in the flowing sands, he would terrorize the villagers.

belonging to the heavenly Queen Mother during the great Peach Banquet. The now-hideous immortal took up residence in the Flowing Sands River. To pass the time, he would terrorize the surrounding villages as well as travelers trying to cross the river.

The immortal Sandy was eventually subdued by Sun Wu Kong and Pigsy when they had to cross the Sands River. After a fierce battle, Sun Wu Kong and Pigsy were able to subdue him. Sandy reluctantly conceded and agreed to join their journey in protecting Tripitaka in their pilgrimage to the West.

Sun Wu Kong "The Monkey King"

The primary individual of Journey is Sun Wu Kong. In fact, because the monkey character is so popular, in some stories that the title "Adventures of the Monkey King," or the "Story of the Monkey King" is used as opposed to "Journey to the West."

The main part of the story revolves around Sun Wu Kong. Other names that followed include the "Monkey King," and the "Great Sage."

As identifiable of the character "Mickey Mouse" is to the Disney Empire, the "Monkey King" is even more popular not only in China, but other parts of Asia as well.

Throughout China one can find a variety of statues, tributes and even characters carved in stone paying homage to the Monkey King of the story of Journey to the West.

Throughout the Journey, the Monkey King, also known as Sun Wu Kong and later referred to as the Great Sage, is a mischievous character that continues to cause havoc wherever he goes.

He is arrogant, inconsiderate, self-centered and delights in breaking the rules. He is also an immortal that carries with him awesome magical powers that he uses to create havoc throughout heaven.

He is however, seen by many as a hero and a character that is fearless, proud and won't back down from what he believes in. He is the protector of his clan and good to his friends.

In Brief: Journey to the West

It is said the Monkey King was born from a mythical stone egg that was magically fertiled by the elements. From a stroke of a lightning bolt, the stone was broken and Sun Wu Kong was born.

Upon his release from the stone, he managed to find a large colony of monkeys who were eager to accept him into their family.

Over the years, Sun Wu Kong gained a yearning for curiosity. On many occasions he would venture off the trail and search the jungle for interesting oddities.

One day he went a little further into the jungle and got lost. It was then when he dared to go behind a waterfall and came to discover a hidden cave. It was huge with a tall ceiling and plenty of room.

The cave was so impressive that Sun Wu Kong thought this would be an ideal location for the colony to move into.

The monkeys were overjoyed at his discovery and how the waterfall provided a canvas of security for the monkeys in order to raise their families

Sun Wu Kong leads the monkey troupe to a secluded home behind the waterfall where they will be free from harm.

without fear.

This earned Sun Wu Kong a great deal of respect from his peers and all the members of the colony. As Sun Wu Kong continued to find new ways to protect his friends in the colony, the elders took notice and bestowed him as their new leader and exalted him as Monkey King.

Appreciating this honor, Sun Wu Kong continued finding new ways to

Though he was heralded
as "King of the Monkeys,"
he was still mortal.

help his friends. In time, Sun Wu Kong realized that he was significantly more intelligent than the rest of the monkeys.

The Monkey King eventually realized that despite his cunningness and dominance over the monkey clan, he was just like them; still vulnerable and still very mortal.

In an effort to go beyond his calling and reach the level of immortality, he decided to leave the colony. Finding a raft, the Monkey King took off down the

The Monkey King set sail on a raft looking for an opportunity to find enlightenment.

river on a valiant search for enlightenment. He didn't know where to go but left it up to the river to lead him. One day, he happened to notice a temple in the foregrounds.

The temple was headed by a Bodhi priest, who was reluctant to let Sun Wu Kong in the door because he wasn't human. Day after day he kept knocking and seeking entrance and he was continually turned away.

However, because of the monkey's determination and perseverance impressed him, the priest finally allowed him in.

The priest allowed Sun Wu Kong to enter because he was impressed by him.

It was through the priest that the monkey received his official name Sun Wu Kong.

At first he was taught how to do small duties, but because Sun Wu Kong was so eager to learn, the priest taught him how to speak and understand.

His thirst for knowledge continued as the Bodhi decided to introduce him to the magical arts. His curiosity impressed the priest so much that he took him aside and began teaching and guiding him through a variety of mystical arts.

Sun Wu Kong soon acquired the powers of shapeshifting, known as the

"72 transformations", an extremely difficult set of skills that allowed him to transform into every possible form of existence, including people and objects.

He also learned to master cloud-traveling, including a technique called the cloud somersaulting in which he was able to travel for many kilometers in single flip. Through the priest, the Monkey King began to also acquire human mannerisms.

But like a monkey, Sun Wu Kong kept getting into more mischief and

Sun Wu Kong is shown by his teacher how to walk on the clouds..

became so proud of his abilities that he began boasting to the other disciples. Bodhi was not happy with this, and as a result, cast him out of the temple. However, before they parted ways, Bodhi made Sun Wu Kong promise never to tell anyone how he acquired his powers.

Sun Wu Kong continued to practice all that he had learned. His magical skills quickly became quite powerful. In time, he returned to the colony and all his friends were delighted by his skill.

Sun Wu Kong appears so intimidating with his new weapon that the other creatures become afraid of him.

Sun Wu Kong wipes his name as well as all his friends from the Book of Life and Deaath.

The monkeys insisted that Sun Wu Kong should acquire a weapon that would compliment his great skill.

Some stories say his weapon of choice was a staff was made of gold, others tell of a staff of silver and some say the staff is silver with gold tips on each end.

The staff was buried deep in the ocean and Sun Wu Kong discovered it during one of his ventures. When the Monkey King grabbed the staff and pulled it from the ocean floor, the staff began to glow, indicating it had found its true master. However, some stories go into more detail and note that the Dragon King reluctantly provided Sun Wu Kong with a twenty foot iron rod which trans-formed itself when touched by the Monkey King.

The staff has numerous magical powers and abilities. It had the ability to be extended to great lengths and in a moment's notice, shrink itself so small that the Monkey King would hide it by tucking it behind his ear.

Using his magical staff, Sun Wu Kong was able to defeat the dragons of the four seas and forced them to give him their best magical armor: a golden chain mail, a phoenix-feather cap, and cloud-walking boots. With his staff, Sun

The Monkey King is summoned by the Emperor to honor him, however, in reality, the Jade Emperor plans to betray him.

Wu Kong then defied Hell's attempts to collect his soul. Instead of reincarnating like all other living beings, he not only wiped his name out of the "Book of Life and Death", but also scraped out the names of all the other monkeys that were his friends in the colony.

Impressed by the monkey's abilities, Sun Wu Kong was invited by the Jade Emperor into Heaven to award him the title of "Great Sage," thus providing him with his ultimate goal, immortalization. Because Sun Wu Kong was still getting into trouble, the Jade Emperor had hoped this new position would help keep him on a short leash and minimize the amount of mischief... unfortunately, it didn't.

Thinking he would have a place of honor with the other gods, the Jade Emperor actually made him head of the Heavenly Stables to watch over the horses. Sun Wu Kong thought this role was one of distinction and honor and gladly accepted. However, when he found out that his assignment was considered the worst position in heaven, Sun Wu Kong was furious and caused havoc all over the kingdom. He was so infuriated with the Jade Emperor that he aligned himself with some of the most powerful demons on Earth.

He became so out of control that the Jade Emperor appealed to Buddha for help. When Buddha met with the Monkey King and made him a bet with that he could not escape from his palm. Sun Wu Kong, knowing that he could cover 108,000 li in one leap, smugly agreed. He took a great leap and then flew to the end of the world in seconds. Nothing was visible except for five pillars, and Su Wu Kong surmised that he had reached the ends of Heaven. To prove his trail,

The Monkey King thought he had traveled clear across the heavens only to learn that he had not even left the space of buddha's palm.

he marked the pillars. Afterwards, he leaped back and landed in Buddha's palm.

Letting arrogance take hold, the Monkey King proudly looked at Buddha thinking he easily won the bet. However, when Sun Wu Kong looked around him, he discovered to find that the five "pillars" he had written his name on were in fact the five fingers of the Buddha's hand.

When Sun Wu Kong tried to escape, Buddha turned his hand into a mountain, sealed him and imprisoned him under the mountain for five centuries. Buddha called the mountain, the Five Finger Mountain.

After 500 years the Monkey King was saved by the monk Xuan Zang who took him as one of his disciples and protectors in his pilgrimage West.

To keep the Monkey King under control, the monk placed a golden band around Sun Wu Kong's head which could not be removed until the journey's end. The monk would tighten the band with a chant when the Monkey was getting out of control.

Sun Wu Kong agreed to help the priest on his travel in exchange for his freedom.

Throughout the epic Journey to the West, Sun Wu Kong faithfully helped Tripikata on his passage from India. Joined by "Pigsy" and "Sandy", both of whom agreed to accompany the priest in order to atone for their previous crimes. Even the priest's horse was

Sun Wu Kong was released from the Five Finger Mountain so that he could atone his sins.

In 1960, Japan also embarked on creating an animation based on Journey to the West. Calling it Alakazam the Great! The series was also known as Saiyu-ki, the Enchanted Monkey and The Magic Land of Alakazam.

in fact a dragon prince. Sun Wu Kong was given free access to the powers of heaven to combat any demons that would get in their way. Altogether, the courageous group encountered a series of eighty-one tribulations and fighting off a multitude of demons before accomplishing their mission and returning safely to and from China.

Eventually, they all became friends and Tripikata performed his duties of successfully becoming their mentor and

A Chinese animation produced by the Shanghai Cartoon Production company. Here you see Sun Wu Kong riding in the clouds with the golden band placed around his head that the monk used to keep control of him.

keeping the documents safe.

The Monkey King, Sun Wu Kong, was granted Buddhahood for his service and strength.

Summary

Though the style of the characters change a little here and there, the overall story of "Journey to the West" remains the same. Here is another animation of the folktale.

Obviously, learning Monkey kung fu will not provide the practitioner with magical powers such as cloud walking, incredible leaping or hiding a silver staff behind the ear. However, one can see how Grand Master Kou Sze admired the folklore so much that he named his new found style after him.

For clarification on the name: The monkey, born from the stone egg, was called the "Monkey King" by his own clan. When he traveled to the temple, the priest gave him a human name, Sun Wu Kong. When he was granted immortality by the Jade Emperor, he was then named the "Great Sage."

Tai Shing refers to the Great Sage.

About the Author

Grand Master Michael Matsuda

Grand Master Michael Matsuda is the only 6th Generation Master and successor to the art of Monkey kung fu in America. He is only the second non-Chinese to completely master the Monkey art. He began his training in 1968, studied Hung Gar kung fu in the early 1970s and began learning Monkey kung fu in 1975.

He is considered one of America's leading authority on Monkey kung fu and is also one of the leading historians on the art as well. He was the principal co-author of two Monkey kung fu books, has over 50 published articles on the art and is recognized by the martial arts community as the leader in America for spreading the art.

In 2004, his accomplishments for opening the doors to Monkey kung fu in America have earned him an induction into the Martial Arts History Museum's Hall of Fame. Today, his uniform can be found on display in the Museum. Matsuda currently teaches in Burbank, CA.

He is a pioneer and has returned the arts to its core teaching originally designed by Grand Master Kou Sze.

Sifu Lyle Fujioka

Mario Prado

Credits

Photography

Mario Prado

Richard Mikado

Michael Matsuda

Karen Gonzalez

Greg Smith

Angela Martinez

Robert Barnhart

Cornell University East Asian Program

Marc Lawrence

The Disney Channel

Mike Swain

Master Matsuda performing in Little Tokyo

Practicing in the hills

Information

Monkey Kung Fu

www.Monkeykungfu.com

(Official Monkey Kung Fu Website)

U.S. Tai Shing Pek Kwar Association

www.Monkeykungfu.com

Special Thanks

Fariborz Azhakh

Doug and Carrie Wong

Dave Burgett

C.J. Martinez

Drew Smith

Josh Freedman

Mitch Norris

Adam Kirk

Cameron Dann

Charity Combs

Ariel Towery

Dominic Towery

Mozes Mudd

Valencia Martial Arts

Cecil and Noemi Peoples

Bob Niitsuma

Craig "Sonny" Iwami

Paul Hickey

Joan, Rafael & Jade Kosche

Angel Velazquez

Luke Walden

Laurie Baggao

Karen Gonzalez

The Louie Family

Paul Hickey

Solomon Avery

Tom Shemanski

Brian and Nena Matsuda

Richard and Donna Gonzalez

Gail Nitta

David Hickey

Phillip Hickey

Team Karate Centers

Phillip Jennings

Michael Tom

Paul Wee

Mike Tom

Richard Chavez

Joel Lederman

Matthew Lynch

Action Martial Arts Magazine

2005

Master Michael Matsuda

Alan Goldberg's
Martial Arts
Card Series

Original photo
presented by
Grand Master
Chan Sau Chung
to Michael Matsuda

More Special Thanks

White Lotus Kung Fu

Chuck Childers

Mike Oda

Robbie

Sarah Shemanski

Chuck & Esther Walden

Ray Souza

Daniel Jaramillo

Marc Lawrence

Seming Ma

The Valley Martial Arts crew

Buck Sam Kong's

Siu Lum Pai School

Lyle Fujioka

Mario Prado

Hidy Ochiai

Sun Valley Polytechnic High

Al Dacascos

Sifu Warren

Sifu Brain

Grand Master Chan Sau Chung

Bong Soo Han

Alan Horn

Richard Alarcon

Chuck Butler

Don Kobayashi

Ruben Perez

Frank Simplicio

Art Camacho

James Lew

Sol Kaihewalu

The Martinez Family

David Husson

Bobby Ferreira

Sun Valley JACC

Rob O'Niel

Mike Swain

Gene Matsuda

Albert Casal

Virgo Talent

43596719R00124

Made in the USA
Charleston, SC
29 June 2015